Fundraising

FOR THE *Long Haul*

Kim Klein

JOSSEY-BASS
A Wiley Company
www.josseybass.com

Published by

JOSSEY-BASS
A Wiley Company
989 Market Street
San Francisco, CA 94103-1741

www.josseybass.com

Jossey-Bass books and products are available through most bookstores. To contact
Jossey-Bass directly, call (888) 378-2537, fax to (800) 605-2665, or visit our website at
www.josseybass.com.

Substantial discounts on bulk quantities of Jossey-Bass books are available to
corporations, professional associations, and other organizations. For details and
discount information, contact the special sales department at Jossey-Bass.

We at Jossey-Bass strive to use the most environmentally sensitive paper stocks available to
us. Our publications are printed on acid-free recycled stock whenever possible, and our
paper always meets or exceeds minimum GPO and EPA requirements.

ISBN: 0-7879-6173-6

FIRST EDITION
PB Printing   10 9 8 7 6 5 4 3 2

CONTENTS

THE CHARDON PRESS SERIES

Fundamental social change happens when people come together to organize, advocate, and create solutions to injustice. Chardon Press recognizes that communities working for social justice need tools to create and sustain healthy organizations. In an effort to support these organizations, Chardon Press produces materials on fundraising, community organizing, and organizational development. These resources are specifically designed to meet the needs of grassroots nonprofits—organizations that face the unique challenge of promoting change with limited staff, funding, and other resources. We at Chardon Press have adapted traditional techniques to the circumstances of grassroots nonprofits. Chardon Press and Jossey-Bass hope these works help people committed to social justice to build mission-driven organizations that are strong, financially secure, and effective.

Kim Klein, Series Editor

Foreword

When I was a 21-year-old organizer, looking to prove that I had what it takes to fight for change in the real world, my new boss, Gary Delgado, sent me to Knoxville, Tennessee, to learn about fundraising from Kim Klein. From Knoxville, I would hit the road on my first donor recruitment drive. My goal was to raise at least the cost of my trip and to add new donors to our list. When I got to Tennessee, Kim thumped me on the back, presumably to test whether my skin was thick enough to raise money for the movement. She made me laugh, and also made me practice my rap while she drove too fast on country roads and berated the other drivers.

In the thirteen years since, I have been part of a team that has followed Kim's advice and painstakingly reduced our organization's reliance on foundation funding. The Center for Third World Organizing, owned and operated entirely by people of color, speaks militantly about race and power — a threatening combination to most people. Our ability to bring in donors, to raise money from our constituency of individuals and organizations of color, and to turn away foundation-driven opportunities has made it possible for us to survive on the cutting edge of public debates on racial justice and organizing. If foundations stopped supporting us today, we would be able to pay the mortgage on our building and keep the phone lines open. We got to that place by applying the lessons in this book, taking some chances and loosening up our creativity. As Kim had promised, being straightforward, persistent, informed and clear about our work and our vision has paid off. We had plenty of fear, and we got over it.

Kim Klein has been guru to social justice fundraisers for many years. Although she is very funny, as thousands have discovered in her trainings around the country, jokes would never be enough to elevate her to such status. She contributes to the movement a willingness to seek clarity, to beat back the rush of denial we all feel when confronted with the inevitable fear, rejection and feelings of inadequacy that accompany our fundraising tasks. She is able to put those feelings in a context, and teach us how to get beyond them enough and go for the big one. As another very funny friend says "You can see the light at the end of the tunnel, and it ain't the train coming at you!" Kim keeps us focused on that light — the light of service, justice, compassion and discipline. She shows us by her effort, not just by her words, that it is possible to raise the money you need, no matter how marginal you feel or are considered in the larger society.

When I came into this work as a student activist, and decided to stay in as a community organizer, there was no significant social movement in this country. The fight against AIDS had not yet matured. The spontaneous combustion of immigrant youth to fight anti-immigrant public policy was a dozen years away. Urban rebellions over Rodney King and Abner Louima hadn't yet revealed themselves. I admired the hopefulness of my elders in the work, imagining their disappointments in the ultimate results of the anti-war, feminist, and civil rights movements. I heard a lot about the long haul, but I was really too young to understand it. I thought the long haul was the willingness to stick in through tragedies and sacrifices. I thought the revolution would come again, and my resilient heart would be ready for the occasional tough spot. I didn't realize that the long haul would be so boring! And that keeping our spirits up would require serious energy.

Age has brought me some understanding of paradoxes. Indeed, the revolution will come again, and it has already come. Every day, we throw the seeds of a new humanity into the world with our services, our campaigns, our ideas. The long haul requires us to see constant suffering and to relieve it with hope and joy. The long haul means doing what we do, with innovation and change surely, but doing it every day for the rest of humanity's existence on Earth. The revolution will be very, very slow, and blindingly fast. We have to prepare ourselves for both realities. *Fundraising for the Long Haul* is about making that revolution happen, making it ours, and creating the possibility for others to own it too.

Rinku Sen
Center for Third World Organizing

Acknowledgments

Thousands of people and organizations made this book possible. If I were to thank all of them, I would need a second and much larger book. I am very grateful to all the organizations I have worked with and for over the past 24 years; grateful to all the board members, volunteers and staff who shared ideas, confidences, dreams and difficulties with me, and who provided most of the insights in this book. I am especially grateful to those who challenged my thinking on the relationship of culture, race, age, disability, gender and sexual orientation to raising money, as well as those who disagreed with my conclusions or my recommendations, forcing me to sharpen my thoughts.

I do need to mention a few people who helped with my writing this book. Fred Goff, Francis Calputura and Guadalupe Guajardo provided in-depth critical analysis of the first draft. Stephanie Roth read all the drafts and her insights were incorporated as I went along. She also provided much-needed encouragement when I was bogged down or behind schedule. The writing was squeezed in between all the training, consulting, travelling and other writing that I do. Stephanie kept me on track and the fact that I finally finished it is due in large part to her. Credit also goes to my editor, Nancy Adess. Nancy has edited all my writing for more than 20 years. I count on her to make my writing readable and consistent. When I can't think of the right way to say something, I write it as best I can, with total confidence that Nancy will fix it. My assistant, Shelana de Silva, should get a medal for her work on this book. She entered corrections and changes on two drafts, photocopied, printed, and e-mailed drafts and parts of drafts, all the while running interference for me with clients and making me laugh. Shelana's lightheartedness belies her total competence and commitment to social justice.

People who know me know that my acknowledgments could not be complete without mentioning all the animals that have passed my way in the last year while I worked on this book. In addition to our dogs and cats, there are the cats, dogs, horses, rabbits and birds of people I worked with and stayed with, along with the cats and dogs of total strangers I encounter walking down the street. They remind me of the most important of life's lessons—that while we may work for the long haul, all we know for certain is the present moment.

Introduction

WHO THIS BOOK IS FOR

Of course this book is for anyone who finds it useful, but I have a particular audience in mind. It includes those who work with the many thousands of nonprofit groups that have sent people to my workshops over the past two decades as well as people in the five hundred or more groups I have worked with in depth either as a staff person, a board member or a consultant. Let me describe the type of group I have in mind:

Its name is "People" (or some subset: i.e., Women, Youth, Eastside, Seniors etc.) For or Against some type of thing, such as Rent Control, Domestic Violence, Rape, Nuclear War, Pesticides, Free Speech, Forests, Racism, Police Brutality, Independent Living, Theater Arts. It was formed anywhere from 5 to 50 years ago, but has most likely been around for between 10 and 20 years. Its budget is anywhere from $100,000 to $750,000 a year; maybe $1 million if it has large project grants. Its budget has gone up and down over the years, but in general is higher than when it started. It has a variety of funding sources, but is probably still too dependent on a handful of individual donors or foundation grants.

These groups have between two and ten staff people whose pay is undoubtedly below what people of their education and skill could make in larger nonprofits. The groups provide health care benefits, generous vacation and sick leave, and flexible hours. Some even have pension plans. Their offices are small and crowded, reflecting some sacrifice in order to keep rent payments down. While some individual staff may have private offices, these are more in the nature of cubbyholes than true offices. If the office is spacious, it has no windows. If it has windows, it has no view. If it has windows and a view, it is tiny or not close to public transportation. It is rarely wheelchair-accessible. If it has a kitchen, it is filthy, or kept clean by one or two people, usually women, who feel slightly martyred about this role. Books and papers are scattered everywhere, along with piles of publications, newsletters, annual reports, direct mail appeals and so on, that add to the crowded feeling. Posters — many beautiful — denouncing oppression or commemorating successful actions or announcing demonstrations and conferences hang on the walls; some may even be framed.

Sometimes these offices have a lot of plants, reflecting someone's ability to nourish them. These plants get sick or die when that person goes on vacation.

The phone rings often, and people usually take turns answering it. Although they may have an intercom system, the preferred method of announcing a call is to shout across the room or down the hall. There may be a meeting room with a table propped up by boxes. The surface of the table invariably has to be cleared before a meeting can take place. Schedules, message boards, job postings, staff to-do lists and master calendars vie for space on the walls.

There is usually one really good computer and printer. Sometimes each person has her own computer, but more often these resources are shared. The printer/s are always shared. In this era of e-mail, you will rarely find a group where everyone can go online at once. In fact, usually only one computer has a modem. One or two broken computers are kept in a closet or under a table. They have been donated and no one has the heart to get rid of them or the time to figure out what is the matter with them. One person is the repository of computer knowledge, and, in addition to his or her job, is on call to all other staff to solve their computer problems. Similarly, one person (hopefully not the same person) is the repository of all knowledge about where things are, such as more photocopy paper or someone's phone number.

There are a lot of advantages to working for such an organization. First of all, you can dress however you like, which for someone like me who hates dressing up and thought fleetingly of joining the Army just so I would never have to worry about what to wear, is perfect. Also, while everyone is respectful of the furniture, it is not delicate. If you spill coffee on it, you clean it up without the sense that you have just ruined an heirloom. You can sit in one chair and put your feet on another. There is a real air of camaraderie. People bring in cookies, candy and other food to share, and take a genuine interest in each other's lives and work.

These organizations were founded with a deep sense of purpose, and they meet real needs in their communities. These communities may be geographic (neighborhood, country, or world), or a group of people who share an identity but who may be widely scattered. Or an organization's purpose may be defined by a common passion, such as peace or prisoners' rights. The group may serve their community in myriad ways, from service to organizing, education to litigation, theater to think tank.

Almost every group I have worked with has described itself as "unique." Some even added redundant adjectives, calling their group "most unique" or even "totally unique." More modest groups were simply "quite unique" or "pretty unique." Each group did fit the definition of unique, that is, one of a kind. Those I consulted with invariably claimed that I didn't understand what it was like to be where they were from: the Southwest, the South, the Northeast, the Northwest, Hawaii or Alaska. I didn't understand the particular struggles of being rural or urban, marginalized or mainstream, advocating for arts or environment.

Santa Fe, Taos, Burlington, Eugene, Boulder, Berkeley, Madison and Austin all claimed to have the most nonprofit groups per capita of any town in the United States. I don't know which of these towns actually deserves that honor, and if I did I wouldn't say.

I feel at home in such organizations. Maybe because I have worked in them for a long time, or because I love the overall sense of purpose that pervades their day-to-day work. But in the 1970s and 1980s, I found a lot of people working in these organizations who were really not happy. They resented the low salaries and the high work demands. They felt the progress the group could make was minimal. Most of those people have left by now. Many are doing good work in their own businesses, or in a corporation or a larger nonprofit. They are happier and they bring their old values to their new workplaces. The people who remain in the small nonprofits are either young and have not yet reached the point where they must decide whether to stay or leave, or are those "old-timers" who find all the trade-offs worth it.

A few of us are somewhere in between those who left and those who stayed. I have my own business as a fundraising consultant and I co-own a small publishing company. I sit on the board of three nonprofits (one too many), and from time to time I work in a nonprofit as development staff so I can remember what that is like. There are a variety of reasons that I no longer work full time for a nonprofit, and why I have returned and left again. Overall, I think the main reason I consult to non-profits rather than work in them is that early on I learned a skill that all nonprofits need, and I wanted to share that skill more than I wanted to work on one issue.

I don't pretend that I have enjoyed every group I've worked or consulted with. Some of them were quite dysfunctional. Some I could help and some I couldn't. Many that I helped would have figured out in time what to do, so I probably just saved them some time and from making some mistakes. But I learned from every organization I encountered, and it is that learning that I share here.

In some ways the groups are right: of course I don't understand the particular struggles of every place I have ever been or every issue they are working on. But I believe there are ways to make your struggles work for you, whatever they are. I never met a group that couldn't raise more money, but I have met hundreds that will not be able to raise the amount they truly need. I don't believe you need to spend more time on fundraising, but I do believe you need to figure out ways to be more systematic and disciplined about your fundraising.

If what I have said describes a group you care about, or you are from a young group and you want to avoid the mistakes that can be avoided, or you are just interested in fundraising, this book is for you.

ABOUT THE STORIES IN THIS BOOK

Dozens of different groups are mentioned in this book. People who know me or my work well may be able to recognize some of them. I do not identify any of them by name because many of the groups are described in terms of a problem they were having and I didn't want to violate confidentiality or embarrass them. On the other hand, all groups have problems; problems are nothing to be ashamed of but are simply information about what needs to be done next. Therefore, I have also not identified groups that I use here as good examples because next month they will have some problems, too.

In many instances I have changed a number of details about a group so that it cannot be identified. In a few cases, I have combined two or three groups that had the same issues and told the story as if it happened to one group only. All of the names of the groups and individuals within them have been changed.

I am grateful to all the groups discussed here as well as to the hundreds not discussed for sharing with me their struggles in raising money to create social change. I rely mostly on memory and my personal journals of the time. I have been as accurate as possible, and any errors of fact or omission are obviously mine.

SECTION ONE

You Can Learn from My Mistakes

INTRODUCTION

In 1979, The Youth Project, a foundation that provided technical assistance and financial support to grassroots community organizations, sponsored a program called the Self-Sufficiency Training Project. The project's overall goal was to help grassroots organizations increase their income and decrease their reliance on foundations (for those who had been able to become reliant on foundations). One part of this project was to teach twelve people experienced in grassroots fundraising and working full time for grassroots organizations how to train others about both fundraising and the relationship between fundraising and organizing. The project was nicknamed "Clone Joan" because at that time Joan Flanagan had written the only book for people doing grassroots fundraising, *The Grassroots Fundraising Book*. (Joan has updated this book several times and it remains a classic — see bibliography if you don't already own it.)

I was one of the twelve being trained. Our trainers had a lot of training experience; most of them were community organizers with experience in varying aspects of fundraising. Heather Booth, Karen Thomas, Si Kahn, Hulbert James, Mary Harrington and, of course, Joan Flanagan, provided the training. I still have my notes from that training. They are yellowed, and the edges of the papers are greasy and worn with being handled so often.

One of the most important things I learned during those sessions was from a comment of Si Kahn's: "People learn more from your mistakes than from your successes." In that spirit, this section is devoted to six mistakes, or lessons. They are not my greatest professional failures, but they are mistakes that other people could learn to avoid. They are mistakes I have seen other people make, which gives me some comfort. I prefer to call them lessons because it sounds better than mistakes. Some of these lessons I only needed once, others I have repeated over and over, some as recently as last week. Some lessons are harder to learn than others. My hope is that you will learn them from me, rather than having to learn them from your own experience. This will free you to learn new lessons. Some of these lessons you have already learned, and so you will learn that you are not the first and you are not alone.

LESSON ONE:
The Importance of Prospect Research

Early in my fundraising training I was given the tools for recognizing a prospect. First, the prospect must be known to someone known to our group. Thus, we narrow down from all the people in the world to focus on those people we have access to. Next, we take the people we have access to and focus on those who are GIVERS. We look for people who give money because that is what we want them to do. If we look for people who HAVE money we will find people who have money, which doesn't necessarily mean they are also givers.

If the person is a giver, we look at what they believe in to see if they might be interested in giving some money to our group. What other groups do they give to? What causes seem to move them? What opinions do they express? What do they read or listen to? Finally, we try to determine what amount of money would be appropriate to ask them for. What size gifts have they given to other organizations? Do they give only from income, or do they also have assets they might give? How much money do they seem to give overall? Is this the first time they are giving to us or have they been giving for years and years but giving an amount that is lower than what they seem capable of, given how much they seem to like our group?

This information is carefully recorded. Nothing is written down that is indiscreet or not our business. The information should be verified by more than one person. If someone tells you that a prospect is "worth millions," you try to check it out. My first boss told me to ask two questions about all information on prospects. The first is, "Can this be true?" and the second is, "Really, I am serious. Can this be true?" Over the years, I have realized that he was right. People will tell you things about other people's money that may not be true. So I am careful, but not always.

In the late 1980s, I was the development staff person for a $10 million campaign. The campaign had gone well for the first six months and we had raised $4 million, but for several months it had lagged. I was moving from discouragement to desperation when one of the volunteers on the campaign, Margaret, told me that a woman named Jean who had been giving money to us for several years was a multi-millionaire and heir to a large textile fortune. She and her husband, Seth, had given the organization $10,000 for three years and $25,000 for the past two years. Margaret was sure this woman could give the campaign $1 million.

"How do you know she could give $1 million?" I asked. "She has it," Margaret assured me. "In fact she and her husband are giving $10 million to another group. I have set up a meeting and want you to come and do the asking with me."

Margaret was competent and reliable. She had already gotten two gifts of $50,000 from other donors, so I only asked two other things about this prospect: Do we meet with both Jean and Seth, and if so, what is Seth like? And, does she have any idea how much money we are asking for and why? Margaret assured me the prospect was familiar with and supportive of the campaign. "You can see for yourself she is a generous donor from her previous history. Her husband is a very successful lawyer, but it is her money that they give away. She is a social worker by profession. They are both really nice people." Because Margaret spoke with great assurance and had been successful before, and mostly because I wanted to believe these people could and would like to give $1 million, I asked no further questions.

On the day of the solicitation, Margaret drove us to the prospects' house. She was more nervous than I had seen her before, and she made me promise that I would actually ask for the money. She said, "I know I am the volunteer and should do it, but I have never asked for anything like this amount and just don't trust myself to do it right." I said I would and did not reveal that I too had never asked for $1 million before. My absorption in my own nervousness precluded finding out why Margaret was so jittery. I calmed myself down by imagining what heroes Margaret and I would be if we came in with this gift. Thus I blew my last chance to find out if I really knew enough about these prospects to ask for this amount of money.

We arrived at their large rambling old house situated on two acres of land. Margaret introduced me to Jean and Seth and their two Labradors. They were warm, down-to-earth people, and I started to feel better. Their dogs lay at my feet, and we began the solicitation with small talk about the ride over and about their house. Margaret seemed willing to chatter about all that forever, but I moved the conversation to the campaign. They did know about it and asked a number of good questions. After we had been there about an hour, I felt it was time to close. Margaret told Jean and Seth that she had given the biggest gift of her life to this campaign and that we were looking for that kind of commitment from a few other people.

She looked at me and I looked at them and said, "We don't expect an answer today, but we are hoping you will consider a gift of $1 million."

I could tell by the way that both of their jaws dropped that they had no idea this was coming. The dogs, who had been sleeping by my feet, sat up, looked at me and then moved to their owners. There was silence, except for the sound of dog paws padding across the floor, and soon a slight choking noise from Jean, who finally managed to say, "I don't think we can do anything like that." Margaret seemed catatonic. I instantly saw how careless I had been in my research about them, and tried to rescue the moment with an even more stupid request. "If $1 million is too much, $500,000 would be fine or..." Before I could dig my grave further, her husband, in a gesture for which I will always be grateful, raised his hand to stop me and said, "We'll think about your request." He smiled very warmly and I shut my mouth.

The dogs laid back down and we all laughed a little. The embarrassed silence that followed his comment allowed me to pull my wits together. I decided to follow the old fundraising adage, "If all else fails, try honesty." I said, "I have never asked anyone for this much money before and I don't know what you are supposed to say after you do it." Everyone laughed out loud, and then for the next few minutes Jean and Seth told stories of their most embarrassing moments. Margaret said nothing.

In retrospect, I could see that I made several mistakes. One, I did not find out what group Jean and Seth were giving $10 million to. As it turned out, Seth's law firm was co-signing a loan for $10 million for a low-income housing project in his town. The details of this deal had been in their local paper, which I could have easily found. Next, I did not find out if the $25,000 they had twice given us was their largest gift or a gift they gave to other groups. Margaret or I could have found this out by asking some other organizations. Nor did I check out the story about Jean being an heir to a textile fortune. It turned out that her family was in textiles and that she had inherited $2 million. Finally, I did not ask Margaret to show me any correspondence she had had with them or repeat verbatim any phone calls, so that I could decide how well prepared they were to be asked for such a large amount of money.

Every time I have made a mistake like this it has been because I wanted the money too much, and my greed has overridden my knowledge and common sense.

As mistakes go, this was pretty minor because Jean and Seth were so gracious. They ultimately gave $250,000 over two years, and they have continued to be supportive of this organization. I saw them a few times after our meeting and they were always friendly. A few years later, I heard that someone told them he knew me and admired my fundraising ability. Jean reportedly said, "We must have seen her at the beginning of her career," but, bless her heart, gave no further details.

LESSON TWO:
The Importance of Being Straightforward

Twenty years before my lesson in prospect research, at my first fundraising job, I had the chance to shadow a successful fundraiser in a large urban educational institution by taking a job with the glorified title of "Development Associate." Basically I did whatever my boss asked and, in return, he took me wherever he went.

One day he told me we were going to see a donor to ask for a lead gift of $600,000 for a capital campaign. My boss said that this donor had given that much to our institution before and was just waiting to be asked to give again. He said I could go with him and the chair of the board development committee, who was also a close friend of this donor.

We arrived at the donor's office and sat across from him. A beautiful, table-sized teak desk with nothing on it but a phone separated the three of us from him. After introductions, the donor spoke quickly, "I hate fundraising. I hate being asked for money, but I love your institution, so here is my gift. Why don't we just go out to lunch?" With that, he pushed a check for $50,000 across the expanse. The development chair caught it, looked at it briefly, pushed it in front of me and my boss so we could see it, and then pushed it back to the donor. "We did not come all this way for that much money," he said. My insides did a double flip, but I said nothing. My boss looked impassively at the donor, like this was a normal conversation.

"Well," said the donor after a moment, "start talking." We did (or rather they did — I tried to look intelligent). After forty minutes or so, the donor said, "OK, I'll give $600,000 again. I hope you'll take this check as a first payment." He pushed it across the desk again and laughed. "Of course," said the development chair and then we all went out to lunch (which the donor paid for).

Afterwards I said to the development chair, "How did you know that giving his check back would work out? Because really, that was the rudest thing I have ever seen!" He replied, "This guy likes to think of himself as a leader. He likes to make the first gift, and to make big gifts. He would have been really embarrassed to find out that $50,000 is not a big gift in this campaign, and that friends of his are making bigger gifts. Believe me, he would have been angry if I had just accepted that $50,000. What I did looked rude, but it was really the kindest thing." Hmmm, I thought.

This lesson sat in my brain taking up space to no purpose for many years until I was myself the staff person for a large capital campaign. We had decided to ask all our long-term major donors for gifts that were 10 times their annual gift (a common strategy in figuring out how much someone can give, and one I should have applied to Jean and Seth in the previous lesson). Although not everyone can give that much, and some people can give more, both fundraisers and donors like this formula because everyone is being asked for essentially the same increment, and it is an easy formula to explain and use with volunteers. When you have donors who do not wish to be thought of as wealthy and who go to some length to hide their wealth, putting a formula like this on your request is helpful. First of all, it is sometimes difficult to do research on these people. Sometimes you find out information you can't ethically use. For example, someone tells you, "I know from a confidential conversation that he inherited $5 million, but he doesn't want anyone to know that and you can never let on that I told you that. In fact I shouldn't have told you." That's the kind of information you have to forget because you can't use it.

Our campaign was carefully done. Every prospect got a letter explaining the request and the formula, with the amount they would be asked for. "We'd like to talk with you about making a gift that is 10 times your annual gift of $_____," the letter read. "We imagine you will need to think about such a large request, and we would like to meet with you just to answer questions and explain the campaign more. One of us will call you in a few days to see when a meeting might be possible."

One of the people we wanted to see gave $5,000 annually and so we were asking for $50,000. I sent the letter and followed up with a phone call. The donor, David, was enthusiastic and set up the meeting easily. I went with another staff person who was also a friend of David's. We talked briefly and David said, "Look, I'll save you some time. I love the idea of this campaign and I have decided to give $15,000—$5,000 a year for three years and to continue my annual gift of $5,000." The other staff and I looked at each other. David was smiling and nodding, and I made a split decision not to refer to the letter he had received making clear we were asking for $50,000. We both thanked him, talked for a little longer and left. I had forgotten the lesson of 20 years ago.

A week later, I got a call from David. He was furious with me. "I went to a party and a bunch of other donors were there and they were all talking about how they had decided to give 10 times their annual gift, and what a cool formula that was. I had never heard of that formula. They asked if I had decided what to do, and I told them about my gift and they all looked at me like I hadn't given enough. That's when I realized that 10 times my annual gift would be $50,000, not $15,000. How come you didn't tell me you wanted $50,000?"

I was totally taken aback. "Because," I stammered, "you seemed to have made up your mind, and $15,000 is a sizable gift, and the formula was in the letter I sent ahead of time."

He shot back, "You made me look cheap because you wouldn't tell me what you really wanted."

"I am so sorry. That was really not my intent."

"Sorry? You are sorry? You think sorry fixes something like this? Well, it doesn't!"

By now, feeling thoroughly miserable, I said, "I know it doesn't help, but it is really all I can say. If there is anything else I can do, you should tell me."

"Well," he said. "I am going to give $50,000, but it is not because of your request, and I am going to make it clear to people that it has nothing to do with you or how you are running this campaign." With that, he hung up.

Over the next few days I tried to blame him for what happened. He over-reacted. He is hypersensitive. He would have been just as angry if he intended to give $15,000 and I had pushed for $50,000. And so on. However, it was clear that it didn't matter if any of these things were true of him — what was true of me is that I should have known better from the lesson I saw 20 years earlier. I should have been straightforward with him.

There were three ways I could have done that. First, by remembering that he speaks quickly and decisively and knowing I would need to get the request in before he could make an offer. Second, if I could not get to the close before him, I should have thanked him for his gift and said, "You know we have asked everyone for a gift that is 10 times their annual gift. I think it has been a helpful way for people to think about what they can do. Did you find that helpful?"

This question would enable me to find out if he had decided on his gift based on this formula. For all I knew his answer might have been something like, "Yes, I knew I couldn't commit to $5,000 a year for 10 years, but I could do it for three years, which is how I came to decide on $15,000." Then I would have known that $15,000 was the gift he intended. As it turned out, he probably would have said something like, "What formula?" and we could have gone on from there.

The third way, the way that the development chair did it 20 years ago, would have been for me or the staff person who was with me to say to him, "David, we were hoping for $50,000. Is it possible for you to give $5,000 a year for 10 years?"

I am not really sure what would have been the right thing to say. What I do know is that my decision to simply thank him and go home was really based on a desire to save me — not him — embarrassment. I didn't want to look like I don't know when to quit or how to be gracious. Again, my self-absorption got in the way of thinking about the donor and talking about his interests in a straightforward way.

LESSON THREE:
Practice Makes Perfect— or at least able to do the job

When I train people in how to do fundraising, I find a lot of active resistance. People object to all kinds of things I present: direct mail doesn't work, phoning is too invasive, people don't want strangers asking them for money, and so on. The more anxious the participants are about fundraising, the more exaggerated their objections. "No one answers their phone anymore, so how am I going to get through?" "When you ask someone for money, you never know if it is a good time for them. I mean, what if you ask somebody and it turns out their dog just died?"

But I find the strongest resistance is to practicing asking for money. This resistance is expressed passively. When I announce that we are going to practice the phone call, a fourth of the people get up and leave. When I divide people into groups of three to practice asking in person, most of the groups turn into groups of two. Suddenly everyone has to go to the bathroom or make a phone call or get something from their car. Those who stay often wind up talking about the exercise rather than doing it.

Everyone needs to find out what their limitations are when it comes to asking for money. Some people just need to get over the first hump of asking. After that, they can ask for any amount of money, from a dollar to a million dollars. For others, like me, there is some ceiling past which we cannot go without further work — that is, some amount of money that seems like the most we can possibly ask for. Practicing asking will allow you to find out what your boundary is and help you get past it. People who don't practice probably are not going to ask in real life. If they do, they are likely to mess up.

I know this from my own experience. Early in my career I helped found a shelter for battered women and I helped raise money for it. I had gotten to the point where I could ask for $50, $100, even $1,000. I thought, therefore, I was in the clear. So, in a planning meeting for a fundraising campaign, everyone wanted to practice what they were going to say. I felt this was a waste of my time, so I went home early, saying that I was tired and did not need practice. I had agreed to ask a man who had helped the shelter in a number of ways for $10,000. He had given that much to another domestic violence program and had told a friend that he would be happy to give "a significant gift." I was cool with the idea of asking for $10,000, even though my entire annual salary was $6,000, a decent amount in those days. I had an appointment with him and I decided it would be more efficient if I just went alone (efficiency is another fallacy).

He was a wonderful man. He was about 50, which to my 23-year-old self seemed old, and he was active in a lot of nonprofits. He said he had personal experience with domestic violence because his mother had been beaten by his stepfather. What was most impressive was that he admitted that he had struggled with being violent to his own wife and children and, through counseling, had overcome it. I had heard dozens of people admit to being abused (which can be very difficult), but I had never heard anyone admit to being abusive. After we had talked for an hour, he said, "I know one of the reasons you are here is to raise some money from me."

"Yes," I said, realizing that he was also a dream donor, setting up the request like that. I moved into the close very smoothly. "You have been very generous in the past, and have helped in a lot of ways. Today I am hoping you will consider a gift of ten..." Suddenly weird thoughts careened around my brain: "You can't ask for that much! Do you know how much $10,000 is? A lot!! You shouldn't even be here. Someone closer to this guy in age and ability should be asking him. What are you doing?" After those thoughts, I was almost overcome with an urge to laugh out loud — "$10,000! Right! What an absurd request — you don't even know how much $10,000 is."

The donor stared at me expectantly. I don't really think that much time went by between the start of my sentence and the finish, but it was enough to blow the request. I backed up partway and started over, "I hope you can help with a gift of ten hundred dollars." His look of puzzlement and confusion sent my brain into another round of criticism. "Ten hundred dollars? What kind of a number is that? You nitwit!"

He said, "You have a very folksy way of speaking. I would be happy to give $1,000. I had imagined you would ask for more." He wrote out a check, which saved me from having to look at him for a few minutes. I managed to thank him and raced out of his office, completely flustered and embarrassed. I had found my "ceiling" too late to practice enough to overcome it.

My macho unwillingness to practice had cost the organization as much as $9,000. I have never missed a practice session again. To this day I practice every type of fundraising before I do it — selling raffle tickets, making phone calls, talking to people door-to-door, asking friends, asking strangers. I want to find out if I am going to choke, and I want to be prepared.

LESSON FOUR:
The Pitfalls of Projecting Your Insecurities onto Others

This lesson could also be called, "How I learned I am not the center of the universe," but there might be too much debate as to whether I have really learned that or not.

Most of the people I know, meet or read about (which I know is a tiny fraction of the world's population, but I am going to draw a large conclusion from it anyway) suffer from two things: low self-esteem and a tendency to be self-absorbed. Together, these qualities are a disaster waiting to happen. We don't even have to look at fundraising to see how this works. For example, I can be standing outside my house and see my neighbor. If she doesn't wave, my first thought is perhaps she is angry with me. Notice I make myself the subject — the result of my self-absorption. But notice also my insecurity: I assume I have done something to upset her. The truth is my neighbor didn't see me because she doesn't have her glasses on, and she is not thinking about me because she is thinking about herself and some problems of her own. When asking for money, with all its taboos and mixed messages, putting ourselves — with our self-absorption and our insecurities — at the center of the process can get us in real trouble.

At the battered women's shelter I mentioned in the previous lesson, I occasionally worked on the hotline with Judith, another member of the fundraising committee. Late at night, there were often hours without calls, so we would talk about different ways to raise money. The shelter operated on a tight budget and rarely had more than two months' worth of expenses in hand at any one time. One night, Judith told me that she had inherited $5 million two years earlier when she turned 21. She wanted to use the money for good things, but didn't really want to tell people she had it.

I had never thought about what it would be like to have a lot of money. To realize that in some ways it was a burden was an amazing insight. Judith and I stayed friends and worked on various projects over the years, and she gradually became more public about her money. She gave away a lot of it, and continued to be active in fundraising. I moved from the shelter to work in women's health and our paths crossed often.

I never asked her for money because I didn't want her to think that her money was the basis of our friendship. People often suggested her as a prospect for fund-raising campaigns I was involved in, but I always found an excuse to not be the one asking her for a gift.

One day about five years later, Judith and I had lunch and she revealed that she had been harboring a resentment about me that she wanted to share. I told her I was open to hearing it. (Californians talked like that in the early '80s.) She told me that she felt hurt that I had never asked her to donate to projects I was working on, when she and I went back so many years and I was one of the first people who knew about her inheritance. I felt immediately defensive. How could she say that, I thought, when I had been sparing her from yet another request from a sycophantic friend? I responded, "Well, you could have just given the money. Why do you wait to be asked, like some princess?" She answered right back, "I always wait to be asked because I don't know if people want a gift from me. I thought you had a reason for not wanting my money."

As I looked at her, I saw an insecure little girl, hoping to be chosen for the team, but not wanting to look like she cared. Seeing this, I told her the truth. "I didn't ask you because I didn't want you to think I am your friend because you have money." Her response was one of the most important things anyone has ever said to me: "Let me decide why I think you are my friend. Don't make that decision for me."

Since that day, I have asked Judith for money a number of times. Sometimes she gives it and sometimes she doesn't. Our friendship is stronger as a result of each of us taking care of ourselves and not making up stories about the motives of the other.

LESSON FIVE:
Haste Makes Waste

For much of my adult life, I took pride in the fact that I could do two or more things at once. Not just walk and chew gum, but important things, like drive and read a report, talk on the phone and write thank-you notes, put a mail appeal together while attending a two-day meeting. It took a number of years for me to realize that the reason I had learned to do many things at once was that I took on too much and did not plan my time well. Further, I learned the hard way that while I can walk and chew gum safely, I really shouldn't do two things at once if either of them requires much concentration.

It was October. I was living in Knoxville, Tennessee, and was the sole staff-person for a small foundation that raised money and then gave it away to community organizations all over central Appalachia. I was planning to send a 15,000-piece mailing and had gotten mailing lists from a variety of sources for this purpose. I wanted to send the appeal right away, before the rush of holiday mail distracted the recipients. I felt nervous about the size of this mailing (15,000 pieces is a lot for a small group in a mostly rural environment!). However, since I had done successful small mailings before, I had decided to skip testing this list, which would have been difficult anyway, since it was a composite of a number of lists.

I was late with this appeal — not unusual. I had planned to have the direct mail package ready to go as soon as the lists were finally rounded up, merged and purged. Now, the lists were ready, but my appeal was not. And my days ahead were booked: I had to go to Beckley, West Virginia, (a four-hour drive) for two days, then back to Knoxville for one day and then to Lexington, Kentucky, (a three-hour drive) for two days. No problem for Wonder Woman!

I made some notes about the appeal package on the drive to West Virginia. When I got to the meeting there, I typed the appeal on my laptop computer while looking like I was taking notes. (I also did participate in the meeting.) During the morning break, I called in an order for carrier envelopes and return envelopes, which would be ready when I got back from Kentucky later that week. I lined up a mail house during the lunch break because the mailing was too big for the usual volunteers to do it. In the day between my trip to West Virginia and Kentucky I had a lot of other work to get done: finishing a grant report and getting ready for an event committee meeting. I also met with the designer about the reply device for this appeal and arranged for it to be sent to me for proofreading the next morning before I went to Lexington. At about 9 p.m. I was in my office finishing the appeal letter. I read it over, thought briefly about who I could ask to proofread all of this before it had to be at the printer by noon the next day, and decided it would be faster if I proofread it myself. The next morning, feeling a cold coming on, I went to my office and re-read the letter. It was good enough. The designer brought in the reply device and I approved that. Around noon, I left for Kentucky, with everything at the printer, having arranged for all the printed pieces to be sent straight to the mail house. They were to get the appeal out as soon as they could. The woman at the mail house said, "You don't want to look over the package one last time before it goes out?"

"No, why? Is something the matter with it?"

"I don't think so. It's just that most people like to come for one final look before sending things out."

Well, as you can imagine, the reason this story is here is not because everything went well and we made a lot of money. First of all, part of the appeal was that we had a donor matching every gift of $50 or more received by the end of October. But not only was I late getting the appeal out, I did not factor in the two days the mail house would take, or the time it takes for bulk mail to be delivered. About half of the people got the letter after it was too late to take advantage of this match. I could blame my ¼ of 1% response on that alone, but there were so many other variables that I can't attribute the appeal's failure to just one thing. Because I had not proofread a letter I had written during a meeting and typed out while exhausted, I did not catch this phrase, "We support a wide variety of groups, including those promoting illiteracy." Finally, I had ordered 15,000 return envelopes of the 6 ¾" size, while telling the designer that the reply device would go in an envelope measuring 7 ½", which meant that the response card was too big to fit into the response envelope.

So, a mailing that cost $7,000 brought in 40 new donors who gave about $50 each, for a total of $900. The mailing also brought in about ten letters from people pointing out the various errors and calling into question our competence in various nice and not-so-nice ways. Since the chair of the board had agreed ahead of time that her name could be signed to the letter, she got feedback from people she knew, which was embarrassing to her, and then to me.

In a big city, a mailing like this would probably have done just as badly, but gone unremarked upon. There are so many bad appeals that one more doesn't stand out. However, the lists I was using were of people who didn't necessarily get a lot of mail, and were not jaded about mail appeals. A lot of people on these lists actually read their mail.

The fallout from this appeal lasted for about two months and the chair of the board told me if I ever pulled a stunt like that again, she would make it her life's work to have me fired. I like to think she was kidding.

LESSON SIX:
The Importance of Process

Feminism — the theory, the movement, the questions, the people asking the questions — is what has most shaped my political and personal life. A hallmark of the second wave of feminism in the '70s was the idea of "process," which meant a number of things, but revolved around the belief that a group should take whatever time it needed for everyone to talk a plan through and come to a decision by consensus. Because feminism is such a basic principle to me, you could therefore conclude that I am in favor of process.

It's true that I don't measure everything by whether it is efficient, since I realize that efficiency and effectiveness are not the same. I want everyone to take the time they need to figure out whatever needs to be figured out. I have spent hours in discussions, for example, about whether men should be allowed at a certain meeting, whether to accept money from some awful corporation should they offer it, what direction a project should go, and so on. I have enjoyed many of these meetings and have learned a lot. Nevertheless, one of my many character defects is that I can't stand spending time discussing an idea that is obviously (to me) a good idea, and about which no one seems to have any objections that I consider intelligent. This impatience has caused me to develop a number of efficient strategies to get an idea passed and to move on. These strategies include, but are not limited to:

- making fun of people who are raising questions and thus gradually silencing them
- figuring out ahead of time who will raise the most questions on a particular issue and scheduling the meeting to discuss the topic when she can't come
- raising my voice slightly and allowing a note of irritation to slip in, giving the impression that we have been over this material several times and people need to pay better attention
- challenging the questioners to come up with a better idea

In my defense, I want to point out that none of these behaviors has been consciously cultivated, and the only reason I know that I do these things is because other people have pointed them out. In fact, I am not in favor of this kind of behavior, but only recently did I realize that in addition to whatever personal damage I was doing by bullying people into agreeing with me, I was not actually getting their agreement, and my plan would usually be foiled.

One of the most serious instances of my employing this constellation of behaviors occurred when I persuaded a group I was consulting with to expand their development department from one person to three people. The purpose of this change was to allow the group to raise more money and to launch a capital campaign so they could move into and renovate a building. The problem was that hiring more development people meant (at least in the short term) not hiring more program people. The group was a collective and so made all decisions by consensus in staff meetings that could last for several hours.

The staff of seven had worked together for several years. Some people had worked at this organization for ten years, and no one had worked there fewer than five years. Their work had expanded, and the person in charge of development had done a good job. Through good fundraising and very careful savings they had enough money to hire one more person. My proposal was for them to move one existing program person into development and use their savings to hire another. It was clear (to me, to the development person, and to the staff person we proposed moving into development) that a few more people in development would allow them to grow exponentially. They had outgrown their office (all agreed on that) and the city they worked in had offered to sell them a somewhat run-down former warehouse for $1. It would cost about $100,000 to fix it up properly, but then they would have a huge office space and no rent to pay. The city needed an answer within a month.

I had consulted on fundraising with this group for about two years and they liked me. I presented a written campaign plan, showing how additional staff would increase annual income and allow the capital campaign to proceed. I believed that they would be able to hire another program person in one year.

The five board members agreed to the plan and were willing to help with the capital campaign, but believed the staff collective should work out the details.

The staff raised many questions. What if I were wrong? Was this building the best solution to their need for more space, or should they try to rent an existing space that didn't need to be fixed up? How much staff time would be involved in supervising the renovation of this building? Who would do the program work that needed to be done for a year while they raised enough money to hire a program person? Did the development staff really have to grow from one to three? Could two do the job, so that the money in hand for a new person could be used for a program person? We answered each question thoroughly and patiently. I thought the questions were intelligent and felt the time was well spent. At the end of the meeting, I said, "It seems like we agree that we should proceed on this building."

"No, I don't think so," said one of the staff. "I think we should think about all that has been presented and discuss it again next week. Let's see which board members can come so that as many people as possible are in this discussion because it has serious consequences."

I thought that was fine, and a week passed. At the next meeting, the board members asked the same questions the staff had asked the previous week. They especially focussed on whether they needed to have two more people in development, instead of one. I pointed out that there was no way the workload of the expanded annual effort and a capital campaign could be done by two people. The existing development person already worked far too many hours.

One of the board members said, "Let's not do that capital campaign. Let the building go. We can find other office space that we can move right into. So what if we are paying rent? When you own a building, you have expenses, and it is not clear that the expenses of this warehouse will be that much less than rent." The development staff and I tried to respond to this. I should have known that something was wrong because none of the other staff responded to any of the objections the board members raised, even though these same objections had already been discussed. But I was too busy thinking that I was right.

This meeting concluded with a decision to have yet another meeting to make a final decision. Instead of using a staff meeting for the discussion, they would have a special meeting at a time when everyone could come.

Afterwards, I met with the development director and the proposed development staff assistant. Our conversation started off reasonably enough. We acknowledged that maybe the others were right. This building seemed like a good deal, but maybe we should forget it. The compromise they were proposing was not so terrible. But I was annoyed at having to discuss the whole thing again, and expressed my frustration. This led us into a conversation something like this: What is wrong with these people? They have no vision. They can't think big. Don't they know you have to spend money to make money? We haven't got all the time in the world for them to discuss every detail of every possible consequence. They are going to expect us to raise all this money, while at the same time expecting us to sit in their endless meetings. And so on.

I have since realized that the first sign that I am about to go into my bullying mode is when I set up an "us/them" scenario. We felt embattled and put upon. We felt misunderstood and had no desire to understand any other viewpoint being put forward. The more beleaguered we felt, the more right our position seemed.

The development person set up the next meeting. There were two nights proposed: one night the staff person raising the most questions about our plan couldn't come, and the other night the person proposed for the second development position couldn't come. "Who is more important?" we asked ourselves, and answered, "We are." So we made the final decision without the questioning staff person. She had agreed to abide by whatever decision was made. I gave another presentation, this time with a sense of urgency. We have to let the city know. This building is being handed to us on a silver platter. Other groups would willingly jump at this kind of opportunity. You can't just stay the same — you need to take a great leap forward, and so on. Questions and objections were met with, "We have been over this before." Or, "Why do you keep raising this?" Or, " Without this plan, how do you propose to raise the money you need?" At the end of the meeting, worn out and wanting to go home, the staff had achieved a reluctant consensus: let's go for the new building and the two new staff.

We had "won." Victory, however, was short-lived. Within a week, it was clear that the development department (now two people and getting ready to hire a third) was being isolated from the rest of the staff. Requests for help with fundraising, no matter how small or routine, were met with, "Can't you do that with your expanded staff?"

The organization gave the city the go-ahead and hired a capital campaign consultant. An architect began designing building renovations. However, every detail of the proposed renovation was held up for criticism by members of the staff. When the capital campaign consultant suggested a list of prospects, in what order to approach them and a timeline, the staff raised a number of objections. Some were reasonable: this prospect is in Europe, that prospect is in the middle of a divorce, this other prospect has seasonal affective disorder and cannot be seen until spring. Though the objections were logical, the mood was not. At every meeting concerning the next step for this building, there was tension in the air.

I realized my mistake. People did not really want to move to this building. They felt pressured to do this capital campaign, and it did not make sense to go forward under that circumstance. The staff, including even the development staff, began to worry that too much effort was being put into raising money for a building and too little into doing program work. A staff that had previously shared development work now saw it as a totally separate and time-draining function. This was all because I, as the consultant they trusted and did not wish to disagree with, had not listened closely enough to their objections to figure out what was at the root of them.

Fortunately, this story ends happily. We called an emergency meeting of the staff and board. I said that it seemed that people did not want to move into this building and perhaps I had pushed too hard for a decision that everyone wasn't really ready to make. Various staff expressed their reservations, and after a while, the group concluded that in fact they didn't want the building. A board member suggested telling the city and, since other groups had expressed interest in the building, she thought it would be fairly easy to back out. She offered to handle it. The capital campaign consultant found another campaign almost immediately and did not charge the group a fee for breaking her contract. The architect was paid for the time he had put in, and was then used to help design an office the group decided to rent.

I learned that it doesn't matter if something seems like a good idea; if the people who will be working on it don't like it, they won't do it. If they won't do it, it is obviously not a good idea.

SECTION TWO

How to Have a Healthy Fundraising Program

INTRODUCTION

If you have read the first section, you will either have learned from my mistakes or realized that you could have written the section because you have already made these mistakes. Or, if you are a rare and probably delusional person, you will think that you would never make such stupid mistakes. We are now going to swing from the mistake end of the spectrum to the other end and describe what healthy fundraising looks like. In my fundraising training, I take participants through a model of what a healthy group has in place and then ask them to compare their actual group with the generic model. That model is described here. It will give you a bar to strive for, a point of comparison and contrast and also a sense of how to structure your future plans for your fundraising efforts.

This section describes a healthy fundraising program in a grassroots organization, five years old or more, with enthusiastic and competent fundraising staff. Each chapter discusses a different aspect of such a healthy program. Keep in mind that your group may not fit the model exactly, but it still may be healthy. As the old saying goes, "If it ain't broken, don't fix it." At the same time, make sure you are not fooling yourself when you decide that something recommended in this chapter that is not true for your group is not a problem. And, if you don't meet a recommendation and you agree that this is a problem, make a plan to solve it.

one

The Elements of a Healthy Fundraising Program

Before any plans are set out or any figures are calculated, an organization must answer the question, "How does our group wish to be supported over the long haul?" If you subscribe to the philosophical principles laid out below, the right answer would be, "By a broad base of individual donors, giving varying amounts, and using a wide variety of strategies to solicit these gifts, with a large number of volunteers involved in fundraising, and fundraising integrally involved in program." Here are the reasons — philosophical and practical — that this is the most sensible approach:

Philosophical Reasons to Be Supported by a Broad Base of Donors

1. We wish to be mission-driven. We want to do what needs to be done and say what needs to be said to those who need to be told, without fearing financial repercussions. We recognize the difference between being mission-driven and being donor-driven, staff-driven or foundation-driven.

2. We wish to belong to the community we serve. We are interested in knowing what people who share our beliefs think about our work.

3. We believe that financial support from a wide variety of people is one test of the validity of our work.

4. We believe that maintaining a broad base of donors is the most responsible and fiscally prudent way to finance our organization.

5. We believe that maintaining a broad base of donors furthers our educational, organizing and advocacy goals. This group of people can be called on to come to demonstrations, write letters or engage in other needed actions in addition to giving money.

It is also helpful to list the practical reasons that an organization would want to seek support from a broad base of individuals. Some of these are embedded in the philosophical tenets above, and I hasten to add that I believe philosophy is practical. However, without a deep belief in the importance of doing fundraising this way, practicality degenerates into cynical opportunism or an effort reluctantly and badly done.

Practical Reasons to be Supported by a Broad Base of Donors

1. The vast majority of money given away in the United States (and in every country where giving has been studied) comes from individuals. The majority of that money comes from middle-class, working-class and poor people — in other words, most people. So, if you really want access to money, you will raise it from the people who give it, which fortunately happens to be the majority of people.

2. Financial stability depends on diversity — both in the sources of money and in the number and types of people raising this money.

3. Many of the strategies for raising money apply only or mainly to raising money from individuals — canvassing, direct mail, special events, planned giving.

4. If you want to engage in any kind of electoral politics or want to influence the outcome of legislation, you will have to raise most of your money from individuals. (You will also have to work with a different tax status than a 501(c)3.)

Exceptions

Not every group can or should be supported by a broad base of individual donors. There are some groups that genuinely believe in building a broad base of donors and do that to the best of their ability, but still must rely on foundations or a handful of major donors for most of their funding. These are groups doing work that is unpopular or controversial in the wider community, but still must be done. For example, addressing racism in a mostly white school district with a history of racial segregation, or confronting sexism in some parts of the military, the church or other bastions of male domination, or making sure gays and lesbians aren't discriminated against in housing or jobs — all these activities may well require outside funding because community funding is not available to the extent required to get the job done. The same is true for organizations working in rural communities, where even support from the whole community will not be enough to finance the work (saving family farms, stopping urban sprawl), or groups working in indigent communities. To whatever extent these groups can build and maintain an individual donor base, their efforts to raise money from foundations will be strengthened and their ability to be mission-driven will be more assured.

There is another set of groups that I have recommended not embark on an individual donor program. The following are types of groups or situations in which an individual donor program will not be the most prudent way to raise money:

1. *Groups that are built around one person.* There are hundreds of organizations founded by someone who wanted a vehicle to do his or her charitable work. This person forms a nonprofit, possibly has staff and a board, but is very much in charge of the direction of the organization; in fact, the organization has no real intention of existing after the person leaves. Most obvious in this category are private foundations that spend all their principal in a limited number of years. The donor to the foundation wishes to supervise the programs the foundation undertakes and to hand pick the grantees. The foundation will cease to exist after a certain period of time. There are churches built around ministers, research and writing programs built around one or two researchers or writers, small public-interest law firms built around one lawyer. They do good work, they are not-for-profit, no one gets rich from them, but they are not ongoing organizations. Generally, they are supported by a few individual donors and a few regular foundation or corporate grants.

2. *Groups that are set up to solve a specific problem or address a specific issue which, once solved, will mean the group will dissolve.* Sometimes these groups do not seek formal tax status, but operate under another organization's umbrella. Examples are groups that form to buy a historical landmark or save some ecologically sensitive property, or force the clean-up of a toxic waste site, or promote a large and one-time-only event (like a 100th-year anniversary of a historical event). These groups may raise money from individuals, foundations, corporations, or even government sources, but their fundraising is very limited. The donors are not cultivated for long-term giving, and there is little effort to build relationships with donors.

3. *Groups that go from large project to large project.* They win a large grant, hire temporary staff, do the project, scale down and write another proposal, win another grant and so on. Nonprofits engaged in research or evaluation are often in this category, as are many technical assistance providers.

4. *Groups that are able to make most of their money from fees for service or government entitlements.* There are certain activities that ought to be supported entirely or primarily through tax dollars, such as police services, fire departments, public schools, public hospitals, the postal service and so on. Some of these entities have been forced to get into raising money from non-government sources, but that is not the optimal solution to their lack of funds.

WHAT A HEALTHY FUNDRAISING PROGRAM LOOKS LIKE

Once you have decided how you wish to be supported, you are ready to compare your program against the following list and evaluate where you are doing well and where you want to make improvements. The elements of a healthy fundraising program are then discussed below.

- You know your history.
- You have an annual fundraising goal and a plan to meet it.
- You have a master calendar that shows fundraising as part of the totality of the group's work.
- You have three- to five-year fundraising projections.
- You have a database of prospects and supporters that is easy to use and that provides you with the types of information you need.
- You know who thinks of your group as their favorite, and you work with this set of people regularly.
- You have an ongoing program to acquire, retain and upgrade donors.
- You use all fundraising strategies appropriately.
- Each board member gives money and most of the board members help raise money.
- Organizational culture allows and encourages staff and volunteers to distinguish between what work is urgent and what it is important, and you focus on what is important as much as possible.
- Your budget contains a line item allowing staff, volunteers and board members to attend fundraising and board development trainings and seminars.
- The organization is willing to spend money to solve problems.
- Every year the same number of people working the same amount of time raise more money.
- No one in the organization lies awake worrying about money more than once or twice a year.

Know Your History

Every introductory course in fundraising starts with how to develop a case statement. The case statement tells why you exist (your mission), what you want to accomplish in broad terms (goals) and in specific terms (objectives), what you have done so far (history), who is in the group and what their roles are (structure), and what you spend and how you raise your money (budget). Everyone agrees that such a statement is needed, yet many organizations don't have a case statement, or if they do they can't find it or haven't looked at it in years.

The most common weaknesses in a case statement tend to be in the objectives, and, because accomplished objectives become the group's history, in the history. When an organization has been in existence for more than a few years and the people in it have a vague, weak or non-existent sense of their organizational history, fundraising will really suffer. Donors want to know what you have accomplished, why they should trust you and why they should give money to you. Not surprisingly, the older your group is, the more donors will expect you to have accomplished. If you can't describe your accomplishments in some dramatic detail, you will lose both credibility and money.

Translating objectives into history is fairly easy. There is an acronym that describes an objective, SMART, which stands for Specific, Measurable, Achievable, Realistic and Time-limited. Your history will answer the question posed by SMART: How long did it take you to accomplish the specific plan that you proposed and how did you measure your outcome? If you were able to accomplish what you wanted and you can show the outcome, your plan was obviously realistic and achievable.

Here's an example of not knowing your history: I accompanied a board member of a successful community organization to a meeting with a prospective major donor. The donor said to the board member, "Tell me some things you have done since you started ten years ago."

The board member replied with great enthusiasm, "We have done a lot. We have solved a lot of problems in our community and we have worked really hard."

The prospect tried again, "What kinds of problems does your group tackle?"

"Big ones and little ones," replied the earnest board member. "Schools, hospitals, libraries, you name it."

The prospect, probably not wanting to be rude, just nodded her head. She had no more idea what the group had done than before she asked the question. In fact, this group had done a lot. They had stopped a playground from being built on the site of a defunct factory until the soil could be cleared of dangerous chemicals; they had saved their local library from being shut down by pressuring the city for additional funding; and they had worked with the local hospital to raise money to open a primary care clinic for uninsured people. The stories behind those organizing drives were as interesting as the accomplishments were dramatic. But this board member was new and had not lived through any of these events. She had not read about them, either, because the stories only appeared in fragments as part of mail appeals or were buried in reports to foundations.

One function of a clearly documented history is to help those who join your organization to learn from the successes, failures and processes of those who came before. In writing up the organization's history year after year, you measure what happened against what you planned to have happen, exposing the strengths and weaknesses of your plans.

Another function of the written history is to re-excite board, staff and volunteers about the work. There is nothing like telling some of your history for people to say, "Wow, that was great," or, "We did that? Well, then this other thing is not going to be that hard."

A third function of a written history is to portray the total context: other groups you have worked with, the sentiment of the city newspaper, elected officials, the neighborhood, religious groups and others toward what you were trying to do, where you have run up against unexpected opposition. Knowing all this will make your planning for the future stronger and your objectives more realistic.

Some people tell me that their history exists in the reports they write to foundations. But that is not your official history. You describe your successes to foundations in words that make sense to foundations. While you do not lie in your reports, you may leave out things that went wrong, and you interpret as much as you can positively. People who think these reports present an accurate history have a skewed view of how much work and what kind of work went into accomplishing whatever you were able to accomplish. You need to have a thorough internal history that forms the basis of not only what you write to foundations but also what you say when you give speeches or when you write direct mail appeals.

Groups do exist whose goals, objectives, history, budgets and financial statements are all thoroughly documented and in order for the past ten years. They can see progress, they can see consistent areas of weakness, they can see years when their plans were accomplished and years where the plans had no relationship to what happened. These organizations grow stronger every year, leadership transitions are smooth, board members are involved in fundraising, and a general sense of purpose pervades all their work.

Other Signs of Health

You have an annual fundraising goal. Your fundraising goal reflects the most successful overall design, which is that at least 60% of your budget is projected to come from individual donations; 10% from product sales, fees or contracts; and not more than 30% from foundation or corporate grants. The foundation funding goes to special programs, start-up projects, capital campaigns or to expand existing programs and not to operational expenses. You measure your success toward your goal against your actual income every quarter, so you can see where you are doing well and where you need more effort.

You have a master calendar that shows fundraising as part of the totality of the group's work, and a large copy of this calendar hangs in a central place where it is seen by everyone.

You have three- to five-year fundraising projections. It is particularly important to have a sense of long-range planning for strategies that can take a few years to generate a lot of income, such as large-scale direct mail campaigns or product sales. Three- to five-year projections also allow you not to worry if you rely heavily on one person or source of funds one year, because you have a plan to move away from over-reliance on that source.

You have a database of prospects and donors that is easy to use and easy to learn and that provides you with the types of information you need. There are a lot of myths about fundraising databases, the most insidious of which is that good ones cost a lot. This is simply not true. A number of excellent databases designed for fundraising cost less than $2,000.

Another myth is that it is easier to struggle with the database you have than go to the effort of converting to a new one. If your database does not do the things you want it to do and that you know a database can do, then you are putting good time after bad to keep it.

However, a database is only as good as the data entered into it, so the other part of this sign of health is that your record-keeping is adequate and up to date, and information is written down rather than stored in someone's head. You routinely gather and add information. You have back-up systems, including off-site files and tape back-up of donor records that are never more than one week old.

You segment your donors, so you know which donors think of your organization as their favorite group, and you work with these donors regularly. You are always encouraging donors to be more thoughtful about their

---

What Your Database Should Be Able to Store and Retrieve Easily

■ ■ ■ ■ ■ ■ ■ ■ ■ ■ ■ ■ ■ ■ ■ ■

FOR EVERY DONOR:

- Full name, correctly spelled with preferred title (Mr., Ms., Dr., Your Holiness, etc.)
- Current address where donor prefers to receive mail
- Date, source and amount of first gift
- Date, source and amount of every subsequent gift
- Additional involvement in your organization (e.g. board member, activist, vendor)
- Whether donor responds to written appeals more than once a year
- Whether donor responds to telephone appeals
- Whether you may exchange or rent donor's name and address

ADDITIONAL INFORMATION ABOUT MAJOR DONORS AND MAJOR DONOR PROSPECTS:

- Family (including name of spouse/partner and children)
- Additional work or home addresses
- Special programmatic interests
- Likes or dislikes that affect raising money from this donor
- Other organizations this donor supports: how, and how much
- Names of people in your organization able to contact this donor personally
- History of all contact with this donor

ADDITIONAL INFORMATION YOU MAY WISH TO TRACK ABOUT ALL OR A SUBSET OF YOUR DONORS:

- Willingness to volunteer
- Named our group in their will
- Contacts this donor has that may be helpful to us

---

giving, to help with fundraising as appropriate and to feel that they are an integral part of the success of your organization. As appropriate, donors are invited to give advice, to write letters supporting or opposing proposed policies or legislation, to attend or even present at conferences, to help with mailings, events, office moves and so on.

You have an ongoing program to acquire and retain donors. As part of this program, you know your attrition rate and your acquisition and fulfillment costs. You determine your attrition rate by counting how many of the donors who gave 12–16 months ago are still giving and then calculating the percentage who have dropped out. Your attrition rate should hover at about 33%. If, for example, you had 750 donors 14 months ago, and 500 of those donors have given within the last 13 months, 250 donors were lost or 33% — perfect attrition rate. If you had 750 donors 14 months ago and today you still have 750 donors, you don't know anything about your attrition rate. You may have lost half of the original 750, but then attracted a new group. It is worth the time to figure this out, and your database ought to be able to help you with this; but even if you have to count your retained members by hand, this information is important. (If you do have to count by hand, see the previous point.)

Similarly, you should know your fulfillment costs — that is, the cost of having a donor. Costs of fulfillment usually include thank-you notes, newsletters, premiums, database entry and upkeep, and renewal letters and staff time for these functions. Letters asking for extra gifts are not included because the donor does not expect to get them as part of his or her donation. Fulfillment should cost less than $5 a person annually.

Finally, you know the cost of acquiring a donor, which is the amount of money you spent to get a person to make their first gift. This cost will vary with the fundraising strategy used and the success of that strategy that particular time. Over the course of several years, however, you can average all your costs and get a sense of what your acquisition costs tend to be. Then you can factor them into your budget. This exercise will also help make obvious which acquisition strategies are not yielding very well and need to be dropped.

You use all fundraising strategies appropriately. When planning for fundraising, you always ask, "What is the point of this strategy: Are we trying to get new donors (acquisition)? Are we trying to get donors who have given to renew their gift (retention)? Are we trying to get donors who have given to give more than they have in the past, or to give several times a year (upgrading)?"

Strategies for acquiring, retaining and upgrading donors are part of a master plan. The point of acquiring donors is to replace the ones who have lapsed and to increase your donor base. The point of retaining donors is to have a predictable income stream and to begin identifying donors who might be willing to give more money. The point of upgrading donors is to raise money and to invite people to express their commitment to your group with a big gift. The strategies work together.

Each board member gives money and all board members understand that fundraising is part of their job. In healthy organizations, board members' gifts are not token gifts; they reflect thoughtfulness on each board member's part, as far as you can tell. Furthermore, at least four-fifths of the board actually helps with fundraising in some way, and the rest of the board members keep thinking they will help in the future.

Organizational culture allows and encourages staff and volunteers to distinguish between work that is urgent and work that is important and to focus on what is important. There will always be tasks that don't get done — we want the preponderance of those tasks to be relatively unimportant. The organization is built around good time-management practices: all meetings are necessary and they function around agendas and produce minutes, and work is delegated to a wide variety of people so that no one person is irreplaceably important to the health of the whole group.

Your budget contains a line item that allows staff, volunteers and board members to attend fundraising trainings and seminars. You encourage people to learn new skills and to get the help they need to do their jobs properly.

You are willing to spend money to solve problems. If your computers are antiquated, you spend a short amount of time seeing if you can get new ones donated or funded, but soon you just buy them. If staff are always late because there is no free or inexpensive parking nearby and no reliable public transportation, you move the office or you cover their parking fees in a convenient garage. If the staff regularly can't get to work in the winter because of snow or always have to be leaving early because of a storm and they spend a good deal of time anxiously scanning the sky, you buy laptops, reimburse people for phone calls made from home, and let people work at home. If board members can't come to meetings unless they bring their children, you pay for or you provide childcare.

Every year the same number of people working the same amount of time raise more money. If you are able to increase the number of people involved in fundraising, you will raise exponentially more money. Even though your fundraising may not get easier over time, it will get more lucrative.

No one in the organization lies awake worrying about money more than once or twice a year. People are free to share their worries with each other, and no one person carries the burden of fundraising alone.

two

The Elements of a Healthy Development Office

For many years, the thought of having a development office was ludicrous to me and to most of the grassroots organizations I worked with. We shared desks, typewriters and phones with the rest of the staff in large lofts or old storefronts. Sometimes we had offices in an office building (novel concept), but then we were squashed into little cubicles. I have come to realize the cost of that kind of working environment and I now encourage groups, regardless of how little money they have, to put some of their money toward decent offices for all the staff. While I focus here on development, I believe that all staff need to have space and equipment that enable them do their job as well as they possibly can.

WHAT A HEALTHY DEVELOPMENT OFFICE LOOKS LIKE

- There is a space with a desk, a telephone and a filing cabinet that affords some privacy to the person working there.
- There is a computer that, if not dedicated to fundraising, is available for fundraising use most of the time.
- There is a master calendar hanging in a prominent place where fundraising dates and timelines are clearly marked for all to see.
- There are up-to-date rosters of board members, key volunteers, staff, key donors (major donors who also volunteer, foundation staff, and corporate contacts), vendors you use regularly, media contacts you talk to often and organizations you work with routinely. Everyone in the organization has copies of these rosters and they are posted in another prominent place. People who are in the office regularly (staff or volunteers) are familiar with these names, so that these people generally do not have to explain who they are when they call.

- There is a literature display by the entrance to the office, with copies of the latest newsletter, brochures, annual reports, a copy of your 990 tax form and any other literature for people to buy or to take.
- Paper files with donor information are in a filing cabinet that can be locked, and data files are protected by passwords. Everyone who works in the organization has a clear sense of what information is confidential and what is not or knows who to ask if they are confused.
- Although fundraising is the primary responsibility of one or more people, everyone in the office feels that fundraising is part of what they think about and participate in, and the development staff can ask for help when they need it or, for extra credit, staff may even offer help unsolicited from time to time. The executive director always plays a key role in fundraising, even if there is a well-staffed development department.

A Room (or at least a desk) of One's Own

The first requirement for a healthy development office is for it to exist at all. The fundraising function of an organization, even if it is staffed by volunteers or is part of the job of the only paid person, must still have its own space and its own equipment. How much space, where it is located and how fancy it is will depend on the organization. However, keep in mind that there is a mathematical relationship between money raised and money spent, which means simply this: no money spent will equal no money raised. This is obvious in strategies like direct mail or special events, but is just as important in setting up and maintaining an office.

The key factor in having a healthy development program is integrating fundraising into all the other work of the organization. This means giving the development function the same level of attention in terms of space, salary, time on the agenda and so on that other programs or functions have. It also means seeing donors as part of the constituency you are trying to reach through your work — not as a sidelined group to whom you relate only when you need their money. I have occasionally seen organizations where the development office was nicer and the salaries for development people were actually higher than everyone else's. This is obviously an accident waiting to happen, a sure set-up for resentment and lack of cooperation. However, I have much more often seen the development function sidelined in some way.

Other Signs of Health

Good development people are on the phone a lot, so they need a space where they can easily hear themselves and the party they are talking to. There need to be enough telephone lines into the office so that people can get through to them (as is true for any staff). When development people are not on the phone, they are often writing — thank yous, appeals, newsletters, proposals, reports and so on. They need access to a good computer and printer, preferably one dedicated to development.

When they are not talking on the phone or writing, development people are most often out meeting with people, so they need to know that their papers, database and files are not touched when they are gone. I make this point not because I think other people in the office can't be trusted, but because I have seen many groups make the development director share her desk with a volunteer, or someone who comes in irregularly, like the bookkeeper or a computer consultant. Since the development director is gone a lot, her desk becomes the one that people use, and they pile up everything that's on it and shove it to one side. When the development person returns, she has to take 10 minutes to recreate her work piles before she can begin working.

Master Calendar. The development function needs to be very visible. A Year-at-a-Glance type of calendar that shows board meetings, special events, proposal deadlines, direct mail drops, major donor campaigns, along with the time leading up to each of these helps other people see how much work and lead time go into fundraising. Organizing campaigns, rallies, conferences and any other major program dates should be posted on this calendar too. Being able to put a calendar like this together calls for organizational planning. Too often program plans are tacked onto fundraising deadlines or vice versa, or the two are not planned together at all, leading to periods of intense overwork, as a programmatic event is scheduled the same week as the launch of a major donor campaign.

Current Roster. Organization-wide familiarity with board members, key donors and volunteers, foundation staff and so on is imperative. It is unsettling to be on the board of an organization and not have your name recognized by the person answering the phone, and it can cost needless irritation when the co-chair of the major gifts committee (himself a major donor) is automatically put through to voice mail because the development director is on a call with a friend.

Literature Display. An organization with a healthy development office will radiate a sense of pride about itself. Even if its offices are run down, they will be neat and there will be a display about the organization near the entrance. The display does not have to look professional, but it needs to appear well kept. A table with one yellowing copy of last year's spring newsletter and a dead plant give the appearance of a group that is on its last legs, whether that is true or not. This display is dusted once a week and is attractively maintained. It is obvious how to join the organization, with envelopes for checks on the display and instructions for filling out membership forms and leaving money. People who work in this office (including volunteers) will direct visitors to the display and are comfortable discussing giving options with them.

Ditto for any virtual literature display, such as a Web site. It is maintained, updated and interesting to look at. The site has a clear and obvious icon that allows people to get information on giving money and the benefits for doing so.

Believe it or not, there are organizations that follow most of the recommendations discussed in Chapter One, and so meet most of the criteria for being a healthy organization, yet their development function is unhealthy. Here are some examples of organizations whose functioning only improved once their fundraising was better integrated into the ongoing work of the organization.

CASE STUDIES

Rivertree Independent Living Center

Rivertree Independent Living Center was given a gracious old two-story house as a bequest. It is near downtown and on a bus line. The donor, a former board member, also left enough money to make the building fully wheelchair accessible by installing an elevator and rebuilding the bathrooms and doorways. The Center has converted the upstairs into three living spaces for people using wheelchairs, and uses the downstairs for their offices and meeting rooms. The development office is located in the basement, down a steep flight of stairs in a room with no windows that used to be a pantry, and was even a bomb shelter during the 1950s. The space gives the development director plenty of room and lots of privacy, but has little else to recommend it.

The Center asked me to work with them after losing their third development director in three years. When I questioned having the development office be inaccessible to most of the people in the organization, the executive director, Farrell, who uses crutches and has a hard time getting down the stairs, said, "The previous development directors have had no problem with stairs and nobody else in the organization wants to know that much about fundraising, except that it is happening." Farrell attributed Rivertree's high turnover in development staff to low salaries and the difficulty of raising money for disability rights issues. While both of these factors may play a part, making fundraising isolated and invisible also takes its toll on the many development people who pass through. I agreed to work with them for six months, and made one of the conditions of my work that the development office be moved upstairs and put next to the executive director's office. Farrell resisted this suggestion, saying that there was not enough space and that he didn't want the basement to go unused, and finally asked, "If that office moves up here, will I have to be more involved in fundraising?"

"Is that what you are afraid of?" I asked him. He nodded.

"Then let's say the answer is 'no, you won't.'" I said.

With a look of puzzlement, but relief, he said, "We can make room." A week later, after the new development director was in his new office, I met with him and Farrell. I started by admitting that I hadn't given Farrell a complete answer. "You don't need to be any more involved in development than if the office had stayed in the basement," I stated, "but your level of involvement is unacceptable."

As we talked, Farrell realized that he wouldn't tolerate his attitude toward development — put it out of sight and don't deal with it — if it were directed toward people with disabilities. Further, he realized he had the same fears that most people have about asking for money — rejection, embarrassment, looking needy or pathetic — but they are compounded by his disability: he has felt that people gave Rivertree money because they felt sorry for him. Moreover, other fundraising consultants have suggested that Rivertree create a direct mail campaign with pictures of their most disabled residents in order to "play on the pathetic, helpless thing" as one put it. I reassured Farrell that he does not need to raise money using pictures or language that is offensive and patronizing.

Along with the new development director, I conducted a series of trainings with board and staff on asking for money. We also focussed on how much successful fundraising Farrell and board members had done over the years. Farrell has impressed a lot of people, and Rivertree has a few dozen major donors. Farrell is an excellent organizer and is able to see that his skills in organizing are exactly the skills he can bring to fundraising.

By being more systematic in their fundraising, and consciously integrating fundraising into their work — including having the development office be a visible part of the administration — Rivertree will be able to raise even more money and build stability in their development office.

Western Counties Alliance Against Rape (WCAAR)

WCAAR has a small office in a trailer behind a school. The trailer is divided in half, with the other half housing a tutoring center. Students who are having trouble reading are tutored there for two hours each day right after lunch. WCAAR has two staff, Anna and Tiffany. Tiffany is in charge of development, public relations and an outreach campaign into the schools. Anna conducts trainings for police, lawyers and victim advocates, and also provides technical assistance to rape crisis and counseling centers in the nine counties WCAAR serves. Both Tiffany and Anna spend several hours a day on phone calls, and they find it hard to concentrate when they are both in the office. In addition, they have a number of volunteers, which increases the noise and the density.

Tiffany arranges with the tutoring center to put her desk in their space and use it when the students are not there. She schedules meetings and lunch while the students are using that half of the trailer. For two years, this set-up is functional, if difficult, for both staff. When the subject of moving to a more adequate space comes up, the WCAAR board insists that all extra money raised be put into developing new programs or doing more outreach.

In the third year, the school announces that they need the tutoring center for two two-hour shifts, moving Tiffany out from 8 to 10 and 12 to 2. She works around this schedule until the school adds a third session from 10 to 12. At this point, Anna and Tiffany call me to see if I can help them convince their board that they need a more adequate space. I ask them to keep time logs of what they do each day, in 15-minute increments for one week. I also ask the volunteers to keep track of the time they spend in the office for the same week.

The results show that about 10 hours of Anna's and Tiffany's time each week is spent dealing with the results of this office arrangement: waiting for students who have stayed behind to talk to their tutor to leave, finding places to meet because their office is too crowded, telling volunteers not to come in because there is no room for them, returning calls that come in while Anna and Tiffany are either working at home or, in Tiffany's case, not able to be in her office. "Plus," Anna sighs, "I can't keep track of how much time I lose in taking aspirin for headaches, or having to start a sentence over five times because I have lost my train of thought." The volunteers also report losing time: one says she could come in all of Wednesday afternoons, but there is no room for her. Another says that she spends a lot of time describing where the trailer is to new volunteers, and a former volunteer says she quit because she could not work in "that mayhem."

Although not scientific, our time-documentation project points to a lot of lost time, which means a lot of work not getting done, and, in the case of paid staff, wages wasted. I tell the board that they are not saving any money on this arrangement. The few board members who also volunteer in the office agree, but are afraid they won't be able to raise the money needed for the cost of a move and for increased rent. They don't know if these fears are realistic because no one has estimated what these costs would be. Once that is done, it is clear that the cost of moving and paying more rent will be more than offset by the increased productivity of staff and volunteers, the ability to have more volunteers, and the increased visibility of WCAAR.

WCAAR suffers from a common syndrome — fear of being unable to raise "enough money" (exact amount always undefined) for decent space leads to accommodating inadequate facilities or equipment, until the accommodation is so automatic that no one questions the wisdom of it and price that is being paid.

Once WCAAR sees exactly what moving will cost and how much their increased rent will be, the board agrees to launch a mini-campaign among themselves and key donors to raise the money. They raise $20,000 for the move, including buying new furniture and upgrading the computers, and $5,000 to cover the first nine months of the $600-a-month increase in rent the group will be paying. This is not only the first campaign the board has ever done by themselves, it is the biggest one they have ever done. They are amazed at how much people love WCAAR and how relatively easy it is to raise this money. When the volunteers who work in the office themselves donate $7,500, board members realize just how much the volunteers hated the set-up.

Moving for WCAAR proves to be an important watershed, not just because the new offices are so much better, but because the organization, in the words of the board chair, "decided to act its age." "We are not a little start-up group that has to squeeze every penny, but we were acting like that," she said. "We learned that we have the support of a ten-year-old successful organization, and all we had to do was ask for it."

Fair Wage Policy Forum

Fair Wage Policy Forum is seeking their first development director. The job description calls for someone with "three years or more of experience in a wide variety of fundraising strategies, including but not limited to individuals, foundations, corporations and government. Responsible for annual fund drive, planned giving program, donor database management, foundation research, proposal writing and reports, and the like. Must be able to work from home. Salary DOE."

The two research staff and the executive director each have an office and share a kitchen. Though not fancy, their offices are very nice and they do not want to have to expand their space or divide one of the offices for a development director. They think being able to work at home will make the development job more attractive. They call me because they are having a hard time finding a candidate.

Until now, the three Fair Wage staff have divided development responsibilities. The group has also received a lot of contracts for research work. However, the situation has become untenable, with each person working 60–70 hours a week to fulfill contract work, publish their quarterly journal, and keep up with the subscriptions and memberships that provide the money to sustain them in the increasingly rare times between contracts.

I ask them why they are seeking someone with government and corporate grantseeking experience, or planned giving knowledge, when they are not pursuing those strategies now. "We didn't know what a job description should really look like, so we took one from the *Chronicle of Philanthropy* and adapted it to our group," explains one of the researchers. I then ask, "Would any of you prefer to work at home all the time rather than have an office?" Sheepishly, they each admit they would not.

I explain to them that their job description calls for someone who probably does not exist, especially for the pay they are offering. I further explain that the way they have integrated fundraising into their work is really healthy, except that it is now taking too much time from each of them. Even with a development person, they will still need to help with fundraising, particularly if they want to avoid becoming entirely "researchers for hire." In order for the development person to work effectively, she will need an office at the office.

After some resistance they agree, and reconfigure their offices to create a fourth space. They also rewrite the job description: "Four-year-old research institute seeks to fill a new position of development director. Candidate must be familiar with a wide range of individual donor strategies, particularly membership and major gifts. Familiarity with wage policy issues and subscription fulfillment useful. Salary DOE." Interestingly, this story ends with one of the researchers applying for and getting this job. He realized he would rather be in fundraising than research, and proves very capable.

DECENT SPACE PAYS OFF

All the organizations described here suffered from slightly different problems, but all their problems were related to the failure to integrate fundraising into the ongoing work of the organization. This failure is most obvious with the Independent Living Center, which insured that few people would be helping with fundraising or even know that there was a development office in the building. However it is most extreme with Fair Wage, which sought to remove the integration of fundraising and program work and take fundraising off-site. For WCAAR, the board had to be shown the validity of the idea of adequate work space as a legitimate cost of doing business.

Because people spend their prime-time hours at work and are expected to do their most creative work during those hours, they must have a work environment that supports this. Ironically, this is more true in a small, understaffed nonprofit than a large corporation. In the small nonprofit, if one staff person cannot get her work done, there are no other people to pick up the slack. The work is simply not done. An organization that scrimps on decent office space — desks, chairs, computers, fresh air, some privacy, and so on — will instead spend all the money it thinks it is saving on high staff turnover and lost staff time. Once an organization realizes that it is spending money on its office space, whether the space be bad or good, it usually elects to have decent space.

three

Characteristics of a Healthy Fundraiser

Of course a healthy fundraising program and an adequate office will not help if the person holding the job doesn't know how to take care of himself or doesn't know what kind and amount of work to expect from herself. We complete the trilogy of this section with a discussion of the person who coordinates the fundraising work for a grassroots organization.

WHAT A HEALTHY FUNDRAISER LOOKS LIKE

- You believe that fundraising should be mission-driven, and that fundraising can and should be integrated into the program work of the organization.
- You will not compromise the mission of the organization in order to get money.
- You have a job description.
- You are able to finish your work in 50 hours a week, and you are willing to take some time off when you work more than 50 hours.
- You take a vacation every year and take a few days off from time to time.
- You stay in a job at least three years and not more than ten.
- You volunteer for another organization, either as a board member or in some other capacity.
- You like and respect the executive director and feel liked and respected by that person.
- You are able to motivate board, staff and volunteers to do fundraising and are happy to give credit when they succeed.
- You do not take personally rejection or failure of others to follow through on commitments.
- You attend workshops, read books and periodicals and participate in professional associations in order to improve your skills and learn new ideas.
- You make a plan and implement the plan. You do not procrastinate.

- You are willing to take risks and occasionally fail, and you can admit failure when necessary.
- You make a financial gift to the organization every year.

MISSION-DRIVEN FUNDRAISING

Much of what makes a person a healthy fundraiser is what makes a person a healthy staff person with any job in a nonprofit organization. The person is able to balance setting boundaries with being flexible, able to be a self-starter who also seeks input and advice from others, works well with a team and sees the mission of the organization as the benchmark for any decisions made. Whether you are the executive director, the lead organizer, the bookkeeper, the administrative assistant, the development director, you have another title, or you are some combination of these, you understand that all the work of the organization is based on its mission. The framework that informs all decisions, from what goes in the newsletter to the contents of the agenda for a board meeting to staff salaries and benefits, comes from the mission and the goals of the organization — not from efficiency, popularity, or convenience. Being very strict on this point is the best way to ensure a healthy workplace, happy and hardworking staff and outstanding and important work.

How Answering the Phone Can be a Question of Mission

When an organization fails to be mission-driven it is sometimes because of a large programmatic decision, but more often it is because of a series of small and seemingly inconsequential decisions. In fact, many organizations are quite mission-driven in some ways and not at all in others. The following is an example of using the mission to make every decision.

An organization that provides services to immigrants has a program specifically designed for seniors. Many of these seniors speak very little English, are not literate and did not have a telephone in their country of origin. In an effort to save money, the organization considers replacing their receptionist, who speaks three languages and is a familiar voice to many of the seniors, with voice mail. The phone could be programmed to answer in all three languages and all prompts would also be recorded in the three languages. Though the staff realize it may take time for the clients to get used to the new system, particularly for those who are hard of hearing, they also rationalize that voice mail is something clients should become familiar with.

In their second meeting to discuss this idea the group weighs the pros and cons of going to voice mail against their mission. In doing so, they realize they can't take this step. They want the seniors to have an easy time dealing with their agency and to feel free to call whenever they need to. They want immigrants to feel welcomed to the community and to have the sense that an actual person is actually interested in them and what they need. In the end, they go to three loyal major donors and get the money they need to keep the receptionist.

Other Signs of Health

Like all staff, the fundraiser should have a job description that allows him or her to do the job in 40 to 50 hours a week. Staff should be required to take time off and to improve their skills by attending workshops and conferences, reading, and belonging to appropriate professional organizations.

You Stay in Your Job. The National Society of Fund Raising Executives (NSFRE), the trade association for professional fundraisers, estimates that people leave development jobs every eighteen months. They usually move to another development job, and then to another and then to another. I often encounter development people who believe they could be happy in development if only they worked in a different kind of organization. Over the course of one three-day period recently I had three conversations: a woman working in a solidarity group said she felt fundraising would be so much easier in a service group, such as an alcohol and drug program. "You can tell donors how many people you helped and what exactly happened to them. Solidarity work seems so vague compared to that." A man working in a counseling program for IV drug users told me, "I wish I worked in the arts. No one likes drug addicts or cares what happens to them. Everyone loves the arts — you work with beauty and passion and greatness all the time." The development director of an art museum confided, "I am thinking of getting into social change fundraising, like solidarity work. Arts are so fluffy and unnecessary compared to these revolutionary struggles — you could really raise a lot of money for that kind of work."

I don't know if any of these people left their job, but I know many people do, believing that another issue will be easier or more interesting.

Unless your boss is a controlling, moody, mean person, or the board is utterly incompetent, or the group is dishonest in what it tells donors, you should try to stay in a fundraising job for at least three years. It takes a full year to understand the organization and how best to present it to donors, what strategies work best, and so on. It takes a year for the board and executive director to place full confidence in your ability and trust your judgment. Just as fundraising strategies often take more than one year to reach their stride, so do development directors. Many people leave a job just when it was about to get easier and it was about to get easier because of all the work they had put in to that point.

Some organizations are more difficult to raise money for than others. It depends on a number of variables, including the issues the group addresses, community response to an issue and, most important, how systematically the organization has been raising money over its lifetime. Nonetheless, if you want to raise money for social change, however broadly you define that, changing issues within that universe is not going to make that much difference.

Many of us got into fundraising because we cared deeply about a cause and fundraising became the thing we did to help promote that cause. However, fundraising is a "behind the scenes" activity. If you love the arts, fundraising for an arts program will be rewarding, but not because you will be doing any art. If you believe in saving wilderness, fundraising for the money to buy property or to pressure the government to save acreage will be satisfying, but you will almost never be out in the forest, unless you are showing a donor around. If you want to raise money for groups helping to rebuild countries destroyed by hurricanes, or fund freedom struggles, or help stop militarism, you will do that from your office, and when you leave your office, you will be visiting donors or funders in their homes or offices. Your front lines will not be the art, the wilderness, or the struggling country. Your front lines are the donors it takes to fund change.

However, there are ways to keep in touch with the issue that propelled you to the work. To remain passionate about the work and familiar with it, I recommend that organizations give all the staff and board members a direct sense of the program. Crisis lines staffed by volunteers often require board members and staff to go through the training and take a shift. I have known of administrative staff (including the development director) at a small theater who have walk-on parts in some of the plays or help build the sets whenever possible. I have known development directors to do substitute teaching, deliver meals on wheels, register people to vote, attend demonstrations and testify at public hearings all as part of their job. It is important that development directors know all aspects of the program, preferably through some personal experience, so they can best figure out how to have fundraising be part of all the jobs in the organization.

While people should try to stay at least three years in their job, I also recommend that they don't stay more than ten. You don't want to become an institution yourself. You need to move to other groups and shake yourself up. If you are in the job too long, the job begins to be molded around you and you become harder to replace.

You Like and Respect the Executive Director. The executive director and development director must have a solid working relationship or the fundraising program will flounder. The development director usually reports directly to the executive director and much of the work of visiting donors and funders will fall to the executive director. The fundraising work of the executive director is usually managed by the development director, who is in the odd position of telling the executive director what he or she must do to ensure the success of fundraising, while being supervised by that person. If the executive director is uncomfortable asking for money or does not understand the long-term nature of fundraising, your job will vary from hard to miserable.

On the other hand, if you respect the director and feel respected by the director, your fundraising work will be able to flower. Early on establish regular meeting times with the director and learn what her working style is. Does she like a written outline of what she is to do, or does she prefer to talk a plan through? Is he a hands-off manager, so that you are to create your work and only ask him when you have questions or concerns, or someone who likes to see every letter before it goes out and know what you are doing every day? There are a wide range of healthy workstyles and your style needs to mesh with the executive director's.

The most important element for good working relationships is trust. Does the director trust that you do your best, that you thoroughly evaluate strategies before undertaking them, and that you are good with other people? If he trusts you and you make a mistake, it will just be a mistake and you and he will go on and not make that mistake again. If the director does not trust you, a mistake will become an open sore and will decrease your willingness to take risks. If you trust the director, then when she isn't able to finish the work she agreed to do, you will know that something more pressing came up and both of you will regroup. If you don't trust her, then when she doesn't do something you may interpret that as disrespectful or incompetent. Mutual trust allows for honesty and even confrontation when necessary.

A good working relationship between executive director and development director goes a long way to insuring a healthy fundraising program.

You Volunteer for Other Groups. The success of any fundraising effort is contingent on having reliable, dedicated volunteers. Understanding why people volunteer, what the pressures are on volunteers and how to make volunteer efforts satisfactory is imperative for fundraising professionals. There is no better way to keep the situation of the volunteer in mind than to be one yourself. This will help remind you that it is not always possible to do all you said you would do, or how easy it is to feel left out of the loop of an important decision, or how anxiety can overcome you as you set out to ask someone for money.

Volunteering, especially serving on a board, is also an excellent way to get perspective, to learn about other issues and to express other parts of yourself. It makes the time you put into your own job more effective, allows you to network with others in your community, and is the right thing to do.

You Don't Make Work Too Important. Studies of work habits show that people who consistently work more than 60 hours a week often become irritable and defensive, lower their immune systems, sleep badly and cease to be as productive as they once were. Further, from an organizational point of view, a job that takes 60 hours every week to accomplish is a job that requires another half-time staff person. People who constantly overwork disguise the cost of doing business and make themselves impossible to replace. Although we have often interpreted the comment, "It took two people to replace her," as a compliment to the person who left, we need instead to see it as a result of bad planning and bad work habits.

On the other hand, fundraising is not suited to people who only want to work from 9 to 5, forty hours a week. It requires some weekends, evenings, breakfast meetings, travel and so on. Some weeks are going to require 60 hours of work. The week before the signature special event, the two days before your big board retreat, the week you switch databases, the very end of your major donor campaign, may require long, intense days or weeks. That's why flexibility is important, as well as a clear sense of priorities.

Development has a never-ending quality about it. Few organizations (none that I ever met with) think they have enough money. Money is spent as fast as it is raised, and you always feel you could have raised more if you had only done this or that task longer or better. But you have to set boundaries on your work. Time is your best boundary. Each day, decide when your day will end. Take weekends off and when you have to work weekends, take a weekday off. Make sure the organizational goals are clear and that they can be accomplished in the time allowed. While letting the time you spend on your job stretch somewhat is appropriate, remember, being a rubber band is not in your job description.

You Are Willing to Take Risks and Occasionally Fail. I recently sat on the hiring committee for an organization that was selecting a development director. The most fascinating question asked of the candidates was posed by a board member who is the president of a very successful investment firm. She said to each candidate, "Tell me about your biggest fundraising failure." The first two candidates answered with something that wasn't really their fault. One said that the board had committed to raising an amount of money that was needed by a certain date and then failed to come up with it. The other said that he was never able to get the executive director to go with him to see donors.

The final candidate said, "I persuaded the board of directors to spend $15,000 on a direct mail program that after three years still had not paid for itself." He described pushing the board to agree to spend the money and pleading with the executive director for a go-ahead. He had cast aside all caution, even forgoing testing the lists because he wanted to take advantage of a lot of publicity the group was generating.

The board member then asked this candidate, "What fundraising accomplishment are you most proud of?" He said that following this mail fiasco, he had gotten together with three board members and two other long-time volunteers and they had developed a plan to raise $500,000 for a reserve fund. The executive director was persuaded to go with the plan by the enthusiasm of the board members. They were able to raise the money in one year, while also raising the amount they needed for their annual operating expenses.

After this candidate left the room, the board member who had posed the questions said, "That's our person. Able to spend money, able to admit he is wrong, and able to pick himself up and try something else just as big." The group hired him and he has been superb. Taking risks that involve talking everyone into something they don't want to do is not the hallmark of a good development director, but being willing to work with a team to develop a big project and providing leadership and enthusiasm for that project is. Clearly this person had learned the difference.

You Make Your Own Gift. Many times I have been asked if staff should be expected to give financial donations in the same way that board members are. Certainly, making a financial donation cannot be required of staff without being coercive. And, to some extent, giving the organization you work for money may seem like taking a cut in salary, since it is from that salary that most people will be deriving their gift. But, just as volunteering is important for remembering what it is like to be a volunteer, donating money is important to keep in touch with what it is like to be a donor. Do you feel good about this group? Do you think the group spends your money wisely? Can you honestly ask people to join you in making a gift and believe that the money will be well spent? Development people need to answer affirmatively to all these questions in order to really do their job well.

THE NATURE OF FUNDRAISING

For many full-time development professionals, fundraising presents three big challenges. The first, as the late Henry Rosso, founder of the Fund Raising School, pointed out, is that development is a job with little authority and wide responsibility.

You are ultimately responsible for one of the most needed elements in running your group — money — but you may have little say in what the money should be raised for. You may find yourself defending a decision to a funder or a donor that you don't agree with. Budgets may be created without proper consideration of the fundraising elements required to meet the budget. You may be expected to raise money without spending any money. An organization that has integrated fundraising into its programs, and an organization in which the development director is an integral part of the staff in terms of planning programs, will avoid much of this problem.

The second challenge is that your job performance is usually measured by dollars raised, particularly in organizations unfamiliar with all that goes into creating an ongoing, successful fundraising program. The number of donors acquired, quality of materials, adequate records, thorough research — none of these are taken into account in evaluating your performance if the cash isn't present. If you are really doing your job, you will increasingly rely on your board of directors and other volunteers to actually raise the money from the community. This means that when they do a good job, appropriately, they get the credit, and you must smile graciously and be happy for them. If you are not genuinely happy for them, you are not cut out for this job.

A third challenge is that the time required to make a strategy pay off is not understood. Board members and even the executive director will say, "We could get that money faster from a foundation." Or, "I don't think it is worth having so many little gifts. It takes so long for them to add up to anything." The development director is constantly educating the rest of the organization about the long-term nature of fundraising: to get a grant from a foundation is usually a process that takes six to eight months, and rarely do groups count how much it costs to get the grant in terms of staff time, let alone how much time it will take to report on how the grant money was spent. To get $25 from a person may seem small, but if the person gives money year after year, with only the cost of the newsletter, thank-you note and renewal notice, the return on investment is very high. If that $25 donor eventually gives $50, $100, $1,000, possibly a capital or even a planned gift, the return on investment could be very high.

Many development directors get tired of having to explain this basic principle over and over and are often in the position of fending off unrealistic and get-rich-quick ideas without discouraging the enthusiasm of the idea-maker. "How about a golf tournament? A Sting Concert? Let's get on a talk show! Take out a full page ad in the *New York Times*! Buy an airplane and visit all our donors!" If you get too much in the habit of talking people out of ideas, you may accidentally overlook a really good one. That's what happened with the Penny Change Can idea. After three other groups rejected the idea of putting spare-change cans on local bar counters, an AIDS organization took it up and collected $80,000 in spare change in three months.

Some of this experience changes if you are the director or the only staff person. You have more authority and you are given credit and support for more than just money raised. Of course, you also have even more work.

The solution to these challenges is to accept them as part of the job. Every job has its trade-offs and these are yours. If you are truly successful in the most important part of your fundraising job, which is integrating fundraising into the work of the organization and developing a fundraising team from board members and volunteers, your burden will be shared and lightened. You will also see that these issues of authority and responsibility are ones that most people in nonprofits wrestle with, particularly if they want activists and community leaders to have some ownership over the goals of the organization. And things improve. As the whole organization becomes more familiar with fundraising and more comfortable with it, your position will be evaluated not just on money raised, but on all the aspects that make a good fundraising program.

BEING A FUNDRAISER FOR THE LONG HAUL

As you can see, if you take the initiative, you can make development an interesting job year after year. Find a group where you have some latitude in your decisions and where the organizational culture is collaborative and supportive. Volunteer for other groups to remind yourself that there are often many ways to raise money. Take time away from work to remind yourself that work is important but it is not everything. Above all, remember why you do this work, and be mission-driven yourself.

Common Obstacles
to a Healthy
Fundraising Program

INTRODUCTION

Groups call me every day with one fundraising tale of woe or another:

"Kim, the board won't raise money."

"Kim, we have a terrible problem. We can't raise enough money. Can you help?"

"Kim, we lost our foundation/corporate/government funding. What shall we do?"

Not having money is a terrible problem. Believe me, I have been in organizations that had that problem. But often lack of money is simply a symptom of a deeper problem. A rash on your skin may indicate that something is wrong with your skin, or it may mean that something is wrong with your liver. In each case, the diagnosis and the treatment will be very different.

Groups that have no money may have money problems, or they may have another problem. They may have drifted so far away from their mission that their donors no longer want to give, or the director may have a mixed or bad reputation, or the board may be known to be ineffective, or there may be any number of other organizational problems. Any problem that a group has will always show up in its fundraising, which leads many groups to think that fundraising is their problem.

All organizations have problems. Problems are normal. If you don't have a problem right now, a big one will turn up next week. As Isak Dinesen said, "The reason God made the world round is so that we can't see what's coming."

In this section I discuss a number of problems that groups face as they get to be a few years old. As you read the section, keep in mind that I am not an organizational development expert. I am pleased that organizational development issues are being studied and written about by a number of very smart and insightful people. My insights and advice come from being in fundraising and seeing how organizational problems, even those seemingly tangential to fundraising, affect fundraising. Further, I believe that fundraising is central to the healthy development of an organization and that fundraisers ought to be involved in identifying and solving any organizational problem, even those that don't seem that related. So I allow myself the option of commenting on a number of organizational development problems in this section, some of which have more to do with fundraising than others. Some of these problems can be avoided, some can't be anticipated but can be solved, and some we just have to work around.

Problems must be seen simply as information — about what you are going to have to do next, what you are going to have to learn about and who you are going to have to involve in the solution. See your problems as situations to learn from and ways to get wiser and resolve not to have the same problems over and over.

four

Founder's Syndrome

The process of starting an organization, nurturing it to success and then letting it go to a new generation of leadership is one that eludes most founders. Many feel that, having worked so hard, they should now stay and reap the benefits of their work, as the organization follows a smooth trajectory to success built on their efforts. They fail to understand that for some personalities the greatest satisfaction comes from starting a group, and they should go start something else. They may feel that everything isn't in place just yet, and after "blank" happens (the next hiring, the capital campaign, the reserve fund) it will be time to quit. Certainly, many founders have a lot of anxiety about what they will do next and fear being a has-been as soon as they leave the organization. Many founders don't know where they end and the group begins; they have few friends outside of work and may be afraid of being alone.

People often blame founder's syndrome on the founder. However, blaming anyone here is counterproductive. The founder can only have the power she has because she surrounds herself with people who excuse her behavior on the basis that she is the founder.

We have an idea that because someone starts something, and because they work harder than anyone else during that phase, they should have more power than anyone else — in essence, that because they started the organization, they own it. In certain settings this is true. For example, if a person starts a small business, appoints herself the president of the company and hires people to work for her, then that person should have the most say in how the business is run. However, when somebody starts a nonprofit, which is overseen by a board and operates as a public charity, that person has given up the right of ownership and has chosen a different model.

There are many ways that founder's syndrome debilitates an organization, but three are most common:

1. **The founder is a visionary and is constantly moving the organization to new ideas and programs.** The board often is hard-pressed to keep up with her, but feels compelled to go along.

If this process is not watched carefully, the danger is that the group will move away from its original mission, or take on projects that are simply too big and too ambitious.

2. The founder builds a successful organization. After a few years, due to her leadership and charisma, the group is big and strong. In fact, it is bigger than the founder's ability to run it. The founder lacks the management skills needed in an organization the size hers has become. To make up for the lack of management skills, many founders become "micro-managers." The danger is that the founder will take the organization back down to a size she can manage, and will do her best to keep the group from growing further.

3. The founder works day and night for a few years. No one comes close to working as hard as this person. She accepts low pay and dismal office conditions. She sacrifices personal relationships to her job. Work is everything. At some point, her passion becomes martyrdom. She consistently feels that no one appreciates her and that she "deserves better" from the organization. She demands an ever-higher salary, more benefits, sabbaticals, a nicer office, a secretary. She is no longer creative, simply demanding. No rewards will ever be enough. The danger here is that the group will no longer do good work, but will still take up a space in the nonprofit community so that no other group will form to do the work. No one dares to challenge the founder and everyone simply hopes that she will quit.

I have seen groups where all three factors were present at once, as well as other variations on the founder's syndrome theme. Interestingly, founder's syndrome can be present in people who were not, in fact, the founders. They may be staff or board members who have been in the organization from the beginning or close to it. Founder's syndrome can also exist in several people at once. This is often seen in small groups where a few volunteers or board members form a clique. Nothing can get done without the approval of this group.

The symptoms of founder's syndrome in any one person are varied but they are usually easy to identify. They include the common symptoms of overidentification with one's work, including working long hours, anxiety and paranoia about the work and those doing it, which leads to micro-management, obsession with control and with knowing everything that is going on at all times, refusal to take a vacation or calling in to work during vacations. But they can also include even more dangerous reactions to organizational change: seeing disagreement as disloyalty, raging when outvoted or refusing to be outvoted by bringing a topic up over and over again until it goes her way. At an organizational level, these behaviors beget other symptoms: high turnover of staff and board members, a few people with intense loyalty to the founder who defend her no matter what, staff who feel that they must always tread lightly, and feelings of relief and freedom among staff when the founder is out of the office.

Founder's syndrome obviously has a negative impact on fundraising. In organizations that have development directors, their creativity will be stifled. They may have to defend decisions to donors and funders that they don't agree with, and, more difficult, explain the founder's difficult or irrational behavior. As people have questions about the founder, they may turn to the development director as someone perceived to have the ear of the founder or as someone very close to the founder.

Of all the trials to plague an organization, founder's syndrome is one of the worst because it is so much about personality and so little about organizational structure. Nevertheless, following are a number of ways that founder's syndrome can be addressed organizationally, along with three case studies illustrating how founder's syndrome can play itself out.

ADDRESSING FOUNDER'S SYNDROME

A number of attitudes and actions can help prevent or turn around potentially damaging founder's syndrome behavior. In fact, the following suggestions can prevent most of the problems an organization may face.

1. Assume good intent. This Quaker saying is important in all organizational work and is probably a decent motto for life. Underneath all the problems that anyone in an organization has or creates, lies a shared basic commitment to justice. By believing that ultimately, when pushed, people do want what will best accomplish the mission and goals of the group, you will not be tempted to add to the gossip, plotting, anger and frustration that are so often present in any effort to address founder's syndrome. By each person assuming good intent — good will — on everyone's part, people may rise to that assumption.

2. Examine what you are about to say: Is it true? If true, is it kind? If kind, is it necessary? The Sufis call this the "three gates of speech." In a meeting or when you are with people who are not your closest friends, don't add to the gossip and innuendo, even though that can be temporarily satisfying. Vent your frustration and need to say nasty things with people who aren't immersed in the organization and whom you can trust completely not to repeat what you said.

3. Be proactive. From the day the organization starts, talk about bringing in new leadership. If the idea of turning over leadership is built in from the beginning and has always been part of the plan, the founder will not feel plotted against.

4. Document the problem. Write down incidents as they happen. If you have to confront behaviors, you will have a clear history of when things happened and what went on. Then, if the founder, a board member or another staff person asks for an example of behavior that needs to be changed, it can be provided.

5. Review the organization's case statement and keep in mind that everyone's first loyalty is to the mission of the group. Obviously, people will have personal loyalties and friendships, but these must be secondary to the goals of the organization. The organization itself is secondary to its mission, and sometimes the organization will have to be profoundly changed in order to accomplish the mission.

6. Separate likes and dislikes from serious organizational issues. Let's say you are a board member trying to deal with a founding executive director. The executive director always doodles during meetings when other people are talking, and this seems rude to you and annoys you tremendously. She appears to be bored, and sometimes she gives the impression she is not listening. The director also keeps bringing up a decision she disagreed with, hoping to get it changed. Ask yourself which of these two behaviors is the most important to try to change. Since you will have the most success changing yourself, and the least success changing someone else, concentrate on making sure changes you ask for from someone else are really critical ones. If you ask for too many changes you will get none.

7. Suggest the founder expand her skills. This can be done in the context of upgrading the skills of all the staff and board members. Talented founding staff should not be forced to leave an organization that has outgrown their ability to manage it, when management skills are learnable. The ability to supervise, delegate, evaluate, and hire and fire staff are all skills and can be learned. Except in rare cases, people do not have these abilities, these gifts or talents naturally. Even the smallest and poorest organization (or perhaps especially such a group) should have a line item in its budget to pay for some of this training. In some cases, a training program may be too expensive for the organization to pay the tuition. Foundations, corporations and major donors who have worked with an organization for a while are often amenable to picking up all or part of the tab for this kind of training. Sometimes a case of founder's syndrome has been averted or corrected because the founder got the training she needed.

Dealing with founder's syndrome requires everyone, including the founder, to make some decisions about whether the group will exist past the involvement of the founder. If it will, how will that happen? These can be painful conversations, but, if handled sensitively and even-handedly among board members and staff, they can be freeing to both the founder and everyone else concerned about the welfare of the group.

CASE STUDIES

Mary

A bright, charismatic young woman named Mary believes that people in her community who are homeless and mentally ill are not getting publicly funded social services they are entitled to because they can't negotiate the government system. Mary starts a group whose goal is to ensure that people with mental health problems who qualify for health care, food stamps, housing and other types of welfare can obtain these services. She recruits a number of people who agree with her goals and are also attracted to her energy and passion. Over time, her organization expands to develop programs that place people with mental disabilities into work settings, and many clients are able to find places to live. Her organization is successful and admired.

After seven years of the organization's solid growth and award-winning work, Mary decides the organization should buy an apartment building to provide group housing for a number of its clients. The apartment building would cost $1,550,000. The organization's annual budget is $350,000 and no one in the organization has any experience with running a capital campaign, or, assuming the campaign would be successful, running a group home. The board discusses Mary's proposal at length and concludes that the organization is not in a position to take on such a project. Furious, Mary chides the board, "How can you live with yourselves, knowing that people will continue to live on the street just because you were too cowardly to do the one thing that would help?" She storms out of the meeting. Chastened, the board decides to hire a consultant (who turned out to be me) to assess the feasibility of this project. Mary is mollified.

I begin my work by interviewing board members, then speaking to major donors, foundation program officers, staff, former staff and former board members to assess whether these key players believe this housing project is appropriate for this group and if it is, whether the group can raise the money needed. I discover that in a seven-year-old organization, with 15 board members each serving three-year terms, there are 50 former board members! Most board members have not finished out their term and no board member has ever agreed to a second term. Similarly, there are four staff positions and 10 former staff. Only Mary and one other person have been with the organization more than two years.

When I call individual donors and foundation people and explain what group I am representing, fully 90% of them say, "Oh, Mary's group." All the people I talk to agree that Mary is an amazing person — visionary, energetic, a good fundraiser, passionate, driven. Former staff and former board members add some less complimentary descriptions: Mary is controlling, she has to have her own way, she expects everyone to work as hard as she does, she thinks no one knows more about the issue than she does, and so on. All, however, say in one way or another, "Well, she started the place, and without her it wouldn't exist."

Once I realize that there is very little organization beyond Mary and that people feel the group would not exist without her, it becomes clear that taking on a permanent housing facility would be a disservice to those who might live there. If something happened to Mary, or she simply decided to move on, most of the donors and funders would likely move on as well and the permanent housing might not be permanent. I write in my report:

> It is quite likely that Mary and a small committee of hand-picked volunteers could raise the money needed for this building. In the traditional sense of "feasible," then, this project is feasible. In a larger sense, however, the project is not feasible. First, it would take all of Mary's time and there is no one on staff who can take over the day-to-day running of current programs because there has been no development of staff leadership. The large number of former staff and the historic lack of longevity of staff do not bode well for serving clients during such a capital campaign.
>
> Further, the board is not strong enough to take on such a large project. Several board members are determined to resign if the project moves forward. Given the large number of board resignations in the past seven years, it is clear that resigning has become part of the organizational culture. The board members that had resigned all cited differences with Mary as the reason for their resignation, even while saying how much they admire and respect her.
>
> Before undertaking any more program expansion, let alone a capital campaign, the organization must decide if it wishes to be a freestanding independent organization, or a venue for Mary to do good work.

When Mary first reads this report, she is angry and upset. After long conversations with me, however, she realizes that she does not trust anyone to do the job that she is doing. I recommend that she take some time off to let the organization run without her. She asks the board for a three-month sabbatical, which they grant. During the time Mary is gone, the associate director does an admirable job. When Mary comes back, she resumes her position as the executive director, but with a staff that has experienced being able to make decisions without her.

During Mary's sabbatical, I get the board to agree to some changes also. Board members promise each other not to resign before their terms are up and to engage in a long-range planning process that would allow everyone to examine which areas would be best for the group to expand into — housing, advocacy, public policy.

No one kids themselves that the changes required for this organization to survive will be easy. I visit the board and staff a few months after Mary returns from her sabbatical. They tell me that Mary is still controlling and can be difficult, the board is still sometimes intimidated by her, but she is much more open to disagreement. Mary tells me she feels much better about the organization and about her abilities as a director. The associate director is able to mediate between Mary and the other staff and is also able to give Mary some honest feedback about her behavior. Mary truly believes in the mission of the organization and she is beginning to realize that building an organization requires that she become less important to the group.

This organization will probably survive and grow with or without Mary, because Mary is now able to respond positively to criticism and the board and staff are learning to practice the rule of assuming good intent. The associate director is modeling excellent behavior — honest and straightforward. This allows, and in fact encourages, the other staff to be honest. Mary is able to be more trusting of the group as a team. Through honest feedback and a basic belief that everyone wants what is best for the organization, the board, staff and director are building a solid organization.

Drama in the Drama Group

A group of 10 people start a small theater company. They want to produce works by new artists that explore social justice issues in the form of interesting and entertaining plays. Three of them are actors and want a place to act. Two are playwrights and want to produce their own plays as well as have a chance to collaborate on other plays. The others are theater buffs and want a chance to be in on the ground floor of a theater company.

The group performs several times over the next three years. The money they raise from ticket sales and ads in their program book covers the costs of costumes, props and rental of a performance space. By now an additional 30 to 40 people volunteer to help out in various ways and the group has incorporated as a tax-exempt nonprofit. In its fourth year the work of the group has become more than can reasonably be done by volunteers. One person writes a successful proposal giving the group enough money to hire a staff person for two years.

The group hires Harry, who is one of the original 10 founders, and for the next two years everything is quite successful. Harry is able to raise money and put an office together. The plays continue to be well reviewed. Harry writes some successful proposals and develops relationships with some individual major donors. Money flows in fairly steadily. The organization is now past the point where financial management can be done by balancing the checkbook and making a list of expenses and income every quarter. Although Harry has no financial skills, he is reluctant to spend the money to hire a bookkeeper or accountant, so he tries his best to keep up. Harry's orientation to money is to save it and to do everything as inexpensively as possible. His thriftiness and frugality are commendable but, when mixed with ignorance, can lead to real problems.

Harry hires an assistant named John to help with ticket sales, data entry, answering the phone and so on. He pays John in cash so the organization can save money on taxes, and he records these payments under the category "miscellaneous." Harry has no idea that this is illegal. Some board members think it is unfair to John not to pay into his Social Security benefits and not to provide him with health insurance, but they, too, do not know that a person who works regularly in an office must be put on payroll. John is 21, doesn't care about Social Security payments and would rather have the money in his pocket than spent on benefits.

Harry translates his insecurity about fiscal management into fear that the board does not have confidence in him and begins to resent their questioning his management. For two board meetings in a row, Harry claims he has not had time to put together a financial report, but that "everything is fine." Now a member of the board has read a book about how boards can be more effective and learned that the board needs a treasurer. This person volunteers to take on that job, and the board approves. Harry feels attacked. He questions why the board doesn't trust him. Although board members rush to reassure him that trust isn't the issue, the board meeting ends on a very tense note.

The newly appointed treasurer, Ann, learns about a financial management computer program from a friend who works in a larger nonprofit. Excited, Ann calls Harry to tell him about these programs and to offer to help set one up. She thinks this will solve the problems Harry is having keeping up with financial reports, as well as help him make cash flow projections and budget comparisons. Harry says he doesn't have the time for this "bureaucracy" and "make-work."

Ann tries to understand his viewpoint, but she has also learned from her friend that the theater may get into trouble with the Internal Revenue Service if they don't put John on the payroll. She thinks donors are going to wonder about such a large amount of spending under "miscellaneous" when they publish their Annual Report. Harry says he'll think about it. He is now worried that the board will blame him, and he feels guilty and overworked. He knows he is not good at finances and computer programs, and thinks he will appear inept if he agrees to use this program. Mostly, he doesn't know what to do to manage the organization's finances in a better way.

More and more, Harry backs himself into a corner. When a grant that Harry applied for is approved on the condition that the theater send an audited financial statement, Harry withdraws the grant application and tells the board that the proposal was rejected. But word gets back to the board through a mutual acquaintance of the theater group and the foundation, and matters finally come to a head.

A few board members get together and confront Harry. Because most of these people have been friends for quite a while, they are more confused than angry. Harry concedes that he has been feeling overwhelmed and incompetent for a long time but unable to admit what he didn't know. The board members, although upset, are supportive of him and tell him that he is good at many parts of the job and is not required to know everything. With the help of Ann and a part-time bookkeeper, the organization gets its books in order. They set John up on a salary and begin paying his FICA (Social Security) taxes. John begins to take classes in fiscal management.

In this organization we have an example of founder's syndrome in a person who is not the only founder. When a group goes from being entirely managed by volunteers to having a paid staff, and promotes someone from their ranks, they need to take into account that this person probably doesn't have all the skills required to be a manager. Harry's dilemma is all too common. As time passes, he is required to do more and more things he is not qualified to do and he has less and less time to do the things he joined the theater for and is good at. This saps his self-esteem and that begins the downward spiral into isolation, covering up mistakes and inability to admit he needs help.

The strength of this group in solving the problem is found in the same casualness that led them to hire Harry. All the board members pitch in to help, they are able to confront Harry and he is able to hear them. They basically like and trust each other and are able to figure out what needs to be done.

Over the long term, the theater board needs to reconfigure itself so that there is more expertise among the members. In order for a board to have confidence in the director, the board members must have, among themselves, the knowledge required to run the group, or at least to know that they don't have this knowledge and need to hire someone who does. Bringing in people who know less about theater and more about fiscal management, accounting, fundraising and the like will be important. The group will also have to find staff people who complement Harry's skills.

This group should be fine if they are able to maintain their sense of support for each other and encourage any of their number to ask for help when needed.

Rob and His Friends

In the first two cases the story, up to the time we know about it, ends happily. In this final story, we see a group destroyed by founder's syndrome.

Rob, a young man with a large inheritance, along with four of his wealthy friends, starts a progressive think tank and research organization. They write opinions about public policy, they analyze the economic effects of legislation, and they help organizations through the mazes of producing and interpreting environmental reports and meeting the requirements of other kinds of regulations. Grassroots groups hire them when they need background information on issues, or when they need help thinking through a position on a complicated subject. The group's newsletter is widely read and the group is well respected. As executive director, Rob raises most of the money from family and friends and, over time, from a large subscriber base.

After about five years, Rob and the board realize that they are not "walking the walk" of their progressive values. To do so would mean having more diversity among the people involved with the organization. The board is 95% white and 70% male. Most of the board members are academics and more than half of them have inherited wealth. The 10-person staff reflects more diversity: half the staff are white and half are people of color, with seven women and three men. Three people are gay or lesbian, and one person is disabled. But Rob, the assistant director and the director of research are all white men. The development director is a white woman.

Over the next two years, in a very careful and thoughtful process, several of the original board members rotate off the board and board membership becomes more diverse. The director of research leaves to take a teaching position and a staff researcher, who is an African American woman, is promoted to that position.

These transitions are not always easy, but because they have been done slowly and with a lot of discussion, they go relatively smoothly. Rob is pleased with the progress he and the organization have made in being more in line with their values.

From time to time, the development director and research director, in comparing notes, realize that Rob's program decisions are heavily influenced by five of his friends who are former board members. The research director notes that Rob often sends her to these former board members for ideas and help. The development person realizes that about 50% of the organization's income is from these five people. Rob himself works for only a token salary, which is another contribution. Each of these staff feels uneasy about these people directing from the wings and they mention it to each other every so often, but cannot figure out if this is really a problem. Their day-to-day work is very absorbing and they don't pursue the subject.

In the tenth year of the organization, Rob announces that he is going to leave. Everyone is saddened by this announcement because Rob is creative, bright, warm and easy to work for. The Personnel Committee prepares a job description and opens a search for a new director. There are two final candidates. One is a former board member and friend of Rob's named Edward. An investigative reporter, Edward has researched and written a number of prize-winning stories. The other, Alice, has 10 years of community organizing experience and is well regarded as a strategist and activist. These two have very different qualifications but both are excellent candidates. They are both white. The staff and current board like the idea of the group having a director with more community organizing experience and more contacts in the community, and they choose Alice.

Rob has been careful not to express an opinion, but when Edward is not hired, he feels disrespected. Unlike Rob, Alice has to have a regular salary, so the budget of the group goes up. In seeking extra contributions from some of the former board members, the development director learns that they are all angry about Alice being chosen over Ed. They express their criticism carefully: Alice is not an academic, she has no writing credentials, she is "too grassroots." When the research director asks Rob his advice about an organizing issue, he snaps, "Alice is the grassroots one. How come she doesn't know?"

The next six months are confusing to the staff and board. Rob and the biggest donors, the former board members, are distancing themselves from the group. They are critical of everything Alice does. Since Alice leaves it to the development director to reach out to these people as major donors, she doesn't notice their deteriorating support. However, a budget report six months into her tenure shows a decrease in contributions from individuals. The development director says that she is having a hard time with the biggest donors. She is reluctant to say that they don't seem to like Alice.

The assistant director, who is an old friend of Rob's, is torn between his friends who have taken this dislike to Alice and his feeling that she is doing a good job. The more he hears his friends talk about Alice, the more he begins to see what they mean. She doesn't write very well. She is often late to meetings. She is too casual. She laughs too loudly. The staff talks among themselves about how to improve the situation.

Alice is soon feeling beleaguered. She feels constantly compared unfavorably to Rob and believes that staff are talking about her behind her back (which is true) and that they dislike her (which is not true — ironically, they are trying to figure out how to spare her feelings).

Other major donors and foundation funders get wind of what is happening.

Alice isn't that good, the rumors say. She would be better in a local organization. Requests for donations and funding proposals are turned down. After a year under Alice's leadership, the organization is operating at a deficit. Alice blames the development director, who, infuriated, quits with only a week's notice. Everyone blames Alice for that, including her allies on the staff. As she becomes more embattled, she forgets her community organizing lessons and isolates herself.

The board, which had been much more guided by Rob and his friends than they realized, doesn't know what to do. Over the next year many of them resign or leave at the end of their term. By the beginning of the third year of Alice's tenure, the organization is bankrupt. Board members resign in droves. Alice is named the guilty party by the rumor mill. She quits and moves away. Eventually the group folds.

Obviously, this is a complicated situation, with class and gender politics providing an overlay that cannot be ignored. Rob's geniality and commitment to democracy disguised the fact that he ran the organization like a plantation. When the board members exercised the power they felt they had, they discovered a shadow government in the form of Rob's friends. The development and research directors might have been able to turn the situation around had they realized the full implication of what they were seeing. Alice might have saved herself if she had sought to build alliances with the staff instead of fighting her battles alone.

In this case founder's syndrome was spread over a number of people, who also had tremendous financial leverage in the group. This organization might have been saved if it had had a broader donor base, so that a few donors were not so important. Further, although the group had done a lot of work on its race and gender composition, it had done no work on class issues. The notion that Alice was "too grassroots" reflected a class bias that no one was challenging. The model, started by Rob, of talking to a few people about programs, policies and organizational issues in informal settings, led to a situation in which formal meetings were not where decisions were made. Consequently, there was no central place where all information was shared or where all the cards could be laid on the table. Had the staff been able to talk to Alice instead of about her to each other, they might have been able to find a way to challenge Rob and his friends.

Some groups cannot be saved from founder's syndrome. Perhaps the founder's mark is too deep. Sometimes it seems that the founders derive a certain satisfaction in seeing that the group cannot run without them, and sometimes those left behind do not have the wherewithal to pull the group together and go on. It is also true that not all founders suffer from founder's syndrome, but rarely do we find healthy groups where the founder is still the director after 10 or more years.

The lesson here is that whenever people in an organization, whether they are board or staff, believe that the organization cannot run without a certain person, that person needs to plan to leave. Founder's syndrome is a leadership vacuum. A healthy organization is strong enough to operate regardless of who leaves. One of the many jobs of the founder, of the board members and of the key people in the organization is to build leadership. This is as important as building an endowment or building a donor base, and it has everything to do with fundraising.

five

The Organization Veers Away from Its Mission

An interviewer once asked me, "What kind of nonprofit makes you saddest?" It was an intriguing question. I could think of nonprofits that made me mad and I could think of some sad stories, but the superlative "saddest" made the question hard to answer. I thought of groups that work really hard and still don't raise enough money, of groups whose work is ahead of their time so they don't get the recognition and support they deserve, and of groups that have done excellent work for years and are brought down by one stupid and highly publicized mistake.

But the saddest groups, I concluded, are those that have survived and grown over the years, only to have unconsciously sold their souls and lost sight of their mission. They raise money (not always a lot, showing that selling out is not necessarily profitable) and they sometimes do decent work. But it is not the work the group set out to do and sometimes it is not the work their donors think they are supporting.

While there are many circumstances that lead an organization to lose sight of its mission, the two most common are these: getting into the foundation habit, and trading everything for financial security.

This chapter explores these two stumbling blocks.

THE FOUNDATION HABIT

Some of my best friends work in foundations. In fact, I have been the executive director of a foundation and the endowment coordinator of another. I have sought and accepted grants from foundations. So, my criticism of relying too heavily on foundations comes out of being both a grantseeker and a grantmaker, as well as a long-time observer of nonprofits working for social change.

There are more than 42,000 foundations in the United States. Their grantmaking, for the most part, is traditional, predictable and unlikely, unless by accident, to create any progressive change.

The money to create foundations is diverted from the tax stream, and wealthy donors are allowed to decide for themselves what charitable purpose to promote. Clearly, people who make fortunes and have enough left over to create foundations are people for whom the system is working. They fund institutions that please them, make them feel better about having wealth, and perpetuate the structures that allowed them to get ahead. Private colleges and universities are the main beneficiaries of foundation funding. Health care research; traditional theaters, operas, and museums; private secondary schools; and large social service agencies are also well represented on lists of grants made.

Further, most foundation funding goes to urban areas, so foundations and their grantees tend to be concentrated on the West and East coasts. Every state has a few foundations that support local groups, and an increasing number of community foundations have developed much more sophisticated and broad-ranging local funding, but these remain a small percentage of foundations and of overall foundation funding.

In all, there may be 200–300 liberal-to-progressive foundations, along with dozens of donor-advised programs in community foundations that make grants to progressive organizations. In some communities there are also dozens of small family foundations in which a sympathetic family member can influence funding to groups that are well outside the mainstream. As a result, I have seen some fairly radical groups be heavily supported by a few foundations.

Like all fundraising, foundation fundraising is largely about who you know. As the years have passed, more and more activists have gotten jobs with liberal foundations, and have influenced grantmaking in positive ways. So, even though the odds are against it, it is possible for social justice groups to receive 50% or 75% of their budgets, and sometimes more, from a small constellation of 15 to 25 foundations. And even though all foundations will tell you that they will fund any one group for only a few years, in fact some will support an organization for five, 10 or even 15 years. Sometimes the foundation takes a one- or two-year break and then comes back for another three- or four-year cycle of funding.

If your group has not had this experience, don't get your hopes up. Many organizations doing excellent work have not been able to break into the foundation world. The problem with foundation funding for most groups is that they can't get it because there is not much of it. They spend hours and hours writing proposals, researching foundation sources, even paying proposal writers and researchers to help them, but in the end they come up with little or nothing.

However, if your organization has received any foundation funding, you have a decent chance of continuing to do so, as many foundations will follow once one of their kind has taken a chance on a group. This leads a group into what I call "the foundation habit."

The problem with foundation funding for groups that get it is that it makes them accountable to foundations rather than to their constituency. The old saying, "Who pays the piper calls the tune" applies to all sources of funding. Deciding on where to get money requires answering the question, "Who do we want to belong to? Who do we want to answer to?"

The Attractions

There are many advantages to having a significant portion, or even the majority of funding, coming from foundations, and this is why groups wind up getting into the foundation habit. First, foundations are the only part of the private sector that must give away money. Everything about them is public information — what their assets are, who is on their board, who they give to. Many foundations choose to publish grant guidelines and annual reports about their giving. They delineate what they will fund (for example, schools and health care), what they won't (endowments and conferences) and when they award grants each year. Thanks to organizations like the Foundation Center, information about them is easy to find.

Second, approaching foundations for money may be intimidating, but it does not generally bring up the fears about asking for money that approaching an individual does.

Third, a grant from a foundation is likely to be larger than a donation from an individual. While $5,000 is a small grant, that is a very large gift from a person. So it can seem that for the amount of time put in, money from foundation sources is much greater than that from most other strategies.

Finally, and this may be the most attractive part, seeking foundation funding is almost always a staff function. The staff doesn't need to rely on a fundraising committee, cajole board members into helping, or provide training and hand-holding to volunteers on how to ask for money. There is no need to maintain an extensive database of donors and time is saved on thank-you notes and letters because there are very few of them. Relationships are limited to those between staff and foundation program officers, which provides maximum message control. There is no need to worry about what a garrulous board member or overenthusiastic volunteer might say or promise. While this puts staff people under a lot of pressure, it also gives them a lot of power. Organizations are reluctant to lose or discipline a staff person known to be good at getting grants.

It is easy to see how an organization that succeeds in winning foundation funding can drift to relying on it. If an executive director or development director is good at getting money from foundations, a supportive board is often happy to let them do it. In this circumstance, attempts to get the board and other volunteers to help with fundraising from individuals often seem like more trouble than they are worth. Threats by foundations to stop funding "after next year" don't necessarily materialize if the organization can come up with new program ideas or repackage their regular programming in new ways that are attractive to foundations they have learned how to please.

The Perils

Although the allure of foundation funding is obvious, there are several problems with depending on foundations for a large part of an organization's income. First, foundation funding is not reliable. I have worked with groups that were funded by foundations for 10 or 15 years. Every year, two or three of their funders would say, "This is the last year," or "Next year is the last year." But this never happened, until it did. At some point, a foundation will make good on its promise to cease funding, which can cause a large gap in a group's budget.

Funders talk to each other; sometimes one funder ceasing their giving can have a domino effect. I have seen groups that have relied on foundations for 70% of their budget go to receiving no more than 10% of their budget in a matter of two years, even after years and years of support. Groups that are already five, ten, or 15 years old then have to scramble to build another source of support, particularly if they have only a year or two to do so. Groups that are not able to replace their foundation funding have to make severe cutbacks, suspend operations or even close.

Second, organizations often modify their programs and projects to fit what a foundation is willing to fund. Sometimes these modifications strengthen the program because program officers at foundations can be sophisticated people with good ideas. But even if the modification is a good idea, the group has agreed to it in order to get the funding. The change has not developed organically, and the group will not do the best job it can in implementing the modification.

One of the most frustrating aspects of my experience as a grantmaker was that I rarely had an honest conversation with a grantseeker. As a consultant, I am in the habit of making a lot of suggestions. Groups that are paying me take some suggestions at face value and discuss, modify or disregard others. When I was a grantmaker, however, every suggestion I made was acted on as if it were the best idea ever to come along. No one was going to challenge my suggestions, so I had to learn not to give advice.

Over time, as the executive or development director of an organization develops relationships with foundation staff, a proposal is not even written until the content of the proposal has been agreed on between them. Thus, the programs and projects of an organization can become the decision of two people, with little input from other staff or from the board of the organization, and virtually no input from the constituency. Program ideas brought to the organization by board, volunteers, clients or other staff are judged by the criterion of whether or not a foundation would fund it. Questions of what goals and objectives best serve the mission of the group are subsumed under estimations of what can draw foundation funding; eventually such questions cease altogether.

Abuse of power runs rampant in these situations. The person with the relationships to funders has a huge amount of power. If that person is challenged or disciplined, he or she may threaten to leave. The organization will take enormous steps to keep this from happening. In some cases, this results simply in one person running the show. Sometimes it is more dangerous, as the person demands a higher and higher salary, more and more benefits, and autocratic and occasionally tyrannical supervision of subordinate staff. Ultimately, an organization feels that it cannot survive without this person. Foundation staff will rarely notice these troubles; if they do, they will not voice criticism. If they think there is a problem, they will simply quietly withdraw by turning grants down.

The final reason that over-reliance on foundation funding is perilous is the most important. The way a nonprofit knows whether its mission is a meaningful one is if members of the constituency it claims to serve support the group. If you are an environmental group and no environmentalists give you money, you should question how well you are perceived to be working for the environment. If you are a gay/lesbian advocacy group and you have only a handful of gay/lesbian donors, you should ask yourselves whether your work is meeting a felt need of that community.

Some organizations have been able to work for years without answering this fundamental question of accountability because they have foundation funding. If their constituency is made up of low-income or poor people, for example, the fact that few, if any, poor people give money to the group will be attributed to their lack of funds, not to the organization's failure to address their constituents' issues.

Similarly, foundations will fund research projects documenting that the United States has a disgracefully regressive tax system in which wages for work are taxed at higher rates through income tax than are profits on stock sales through capital gains tax, or that the nation overspends on a large and unwieldy military, or that it uses public funds to subsidize corporate profit. However, they are unlikely to fund groups that are organizing to change these tax laws. As a result, the foundation world gets to look like they are doing a lot for social problems without making any real change at all.

With all of this in mind, even if you can get money from foundations, you need to think seriously about how much of your budget you will take from that source, and how you can ensure that compromises you make in order to get this funding are truly good for your organization. Consider what mechanisms can be put in place to ensure that the organization will be driven by its mission, and not by a funder or the executive director or the desire for security.

Some institutional actions that would help include regularly reviewing funding sources, ensuring that board members and volunteers understand the nature of fundraising and their role in it, and holding retreats in which every program is examined point by point for legitimacy. Most important is an organizational commitment to have those people who are affected by the program be involved as much as possible in creating it. In short, the organization's commitment to its programs and its internal politics must supersede its desire to raise funds, no matter what the cost.

One Group's Adventures with Foundations

Five people start a tenants' rights group in the basement of a church in a poor, run-down neighborhood of a large city. There are two students, two tenants from one particularly awful apartment building, and one long-time housing activist. They target the apartment building of the two tenants and, after unsuccessful efforts to negotiate improvements with the absentee landlord's representative, organize a rent strike. They get a lot of publicity and, after only two months, the landlord agrees to their demands. They go on to another apartment building.

This all-volunteer group raises money by passing the hat at community meetings and tenant meetings. Occasionally their publicity brings in unsolicited donations. They are fiscally sponsored by the church they meet in, and their needs for money are small. One day, the church secretary tells the tenants rights group they have received a grant of $10,000 from a foundation where the husband of the minister of the church sits on the board. The group is ecstatic and overwhelmed. At their next meeting, they discuss how to spend the money. They decide to hire an organizer so they can work in more buildings at one time, and to see if they can get more grants. The person they hire to be a half-time organizer has more experience writing proposals than organizing, so that is what he does. He secures another $45,000 in grant funding.

The organizer starts to work full time and they rent a small store-front office in their neighborhood. The founders continue organizing in two apartment buildings. In both cases, the landlords do not want bad publicity and so make most of the improvements the tenants demand. On the strength of these three successes, the staff person says he thinks they can get money to write a manual on how to do tenant organizing. They can sell the manual and create an income stream. With the group's backing, he seeks funding for the manual project.

The foundation most likely to fund such an enterprise says that the manual would be more useful if there were a research component to it. The research would document what percentage of people live in substandard housing in the area the group serves and contain profiles of the landlords and the tenants (average age, income, family size, family make-up and race). The organizer doesn't see the point of this research; some of it has already been done, and the overall results would probably not be that surprising. However, the foundation says it would be willing to put about $75,000 a year for two years into this research and the manual.

Everyone in the group agrees that there is no point in turning the money down, and they are happy the manual will get written. They hire a research firm, which tells them that the research will not be objective if the group sponsoring the research is also doing the organizing. So, the group agrees not to do any organizing for a few months until the research is completed

There are also changes in the group's make-up. Only two of the founders remain because the students have graduated and left and the housing activist, now with a demanding job, no longer has the time to volunteer for the group. The tenants who are left turn to the organizer for direction. He suggests that the group get its own tax status and board of directors and become independent of the church. He will take the title of Executive Director. They agree.

Meanwhile, a foundation that he had applied to for a community organizing project several months before the research grant came through contacts him to say that they are interested in his proposal but do not like to fund community organizing. They wonder if the group would be willing to change the project to some kind of leadership development training. They apply for and receive a large grant to do leadership development.

At this point the group decides to hire two more staff people and move to a bigger office in a nicer neighborhood. They continue to this day doing research, writing, publishing and training on issues related to community organizing, tenants rights and issues in urban low-income neighborhoods. They no longer organize tenants directly to demand improvements in their living conditions.

SECURITY: THE ULTIMATE TRAP

Let me start with a story. Recently, a shelter for battered women in Oakland called A Safe Place celebrated its twentieth anniversary. I was one of the four women who had founded that shelter, and we were honored at a gala event. The event brought up many memories of my early fundraising adventures with this group, one of which is how we got our first building. It was a great lesson in the opposite of seeking security at any cost.

In the 1970s rents in Oakland were skyrocketing. A lot of organizations were having a hard time finding affordable, decent space, and, since we needed a place with six or seven bedrooms and three or four bathrooms on a busy street near public transportation, we were having a harder time than most. Ideally, our place would also have some kind of fenced yard for the children and a space that could be made into an office. Moreover, we needed a landlord who either was not going to ask too many questions about all the comings and goings, or was going to be supportive of us.

From a property owner's viewpoint, renting to a domestic violence program isn't your smartest financial move. With so many people in and out of the place, the walls and floors tend to be hard used. Occasionally, when an abandoned male partner finds the shelter, there can be a shooting. Even without violence, the neighbors may complain about all the activity.

We searched for a long time and found nothing that would work. Finally, by chance, I met a woman named Carolyn who had just come into a small inheritance. She wanted to help our program financially, but didn't want to give away any of the principal of her money. She thought she might invest the money and donate the interest to the shelter. I thought of something even better: She could buy a building and rent it to us for no more than the payments on the mortgage. This would stabilize our building costs, give us a supportive landlord, and give her an investment that could appreciate in value. Both Carolyn and the Safe Place collective (as we were then organized) were delighted with the plan.

Though happy to help in this way, once Carolyn had purchased the house she was also anxious about our ability to pay the mortgage. I assured her I believed we could meet the payments. We were raising money as fast as we could. I knew we lived on the edge financially and sometimes had to postpone paying our tiny staff, but even so, I believed we could pay the rent.

The week before the first payment was due, we moved in. It was a great set-up for us and we were thrilled. Carolyn called me several times to remind me of the due date for the first payment. The night before we were to have a check to Carolyn by 9 a.m., I went to a meeting at the new office. "I thought I would just take the check to her house tonight," I said, "so that she can stop worrying."

"The problem is that we don't have all the money right now," said the treasurer. "I thought you had some plan for getting the money."

"Me? I have been arranging this building. When would I have had time to get the money? I thought you had a plan for getting this money."

We would have gone on playing "search for the guilty party" for a lot longer, but a sensible member of our collective said, "Whatever anyone thought doesn't matter because we don't have the money and we have about 16 hours to get it, during half of which people will be sleeping. Let's think of something right now."

With that, we made and implemented an immediate plan. There were five of us in the room and we needed $900 (a fortune at that time). We would call all our friends and hope that enough of them were home and feeling generous. One person refused to call, so her job was to drive around and pick up the checks. She called in from pay phones every half hour and we told her where to go next. In the next three hours, we raised the $900, mostly in gifts of $25 and $35, but one generous soul gave $100 and three people gave $50.

When I look back on that experience, I am amazed that both I and the group were so casual about the money we had promised. I wouldn't advise groups to operate like that — in fact now I would think it was irresponsible. Yet that capacity to take big risks, live at the edge and have the confidence that we would pull this out of the water was what allowed us to conceptualize a domestic violence program in the first place. I have lost that confidence to some extent and I feel sad about it. And I feel sorry for my colleagues who have lost it altogether and who now measure every financial move against the litmus test of security.

When Security Rules

Don't get me wrong — security is a good thing. But the desire for it becomes a problem when it overshadows an organization's commitment to its mission.

There are many ways that the search for security can dominate an organization; most of them fall into three categories:

1. The organization insists on a level of financial security that few individuals could ever aspire to. As a result, it amasses more and more money into various kinds of savings — restricted funds, reserve funds, endowments. This type of organization confuses fund raising with fund hoarding.

2. The organization keeps its costs very low and sacrifices quality of work and staff morale to save money. This is the opposite of #1, but comes from the same motive. This type of group confuses fund raising with fund squeezing.

3. The organization drifts into financial security by changing the course of their work to attract funding for projects they did not originally set out to do. They confuse fund raising with fund chasing, as illustrated in the story earlier in this chapter, "One Group's Adventures with Foundations."

It is easy to see why organizations have made security such a high priority. All through the 1990s we read various doomsday scenarios about the ruin of the Social Security program, the imminent collapse of the health care system, and the overload of all social service agencies under the multiple burdens of more people to serve and less money with which to serve them. These articles and news reports often appear side-by-side with stories of our booming economy and lower unemployment statistics. All this conflicting information makes us insecure and makes us want to try to exert some control over our financial futures, both individually and organizationally.

Further, it is much more expensive to run an organization now than it was 10 or 15 years ago. Even tiny organizations have a hard time functioning without computers, fax machines, e-mail and other time- and labor-saving devices (some of which, ironically, have saved neither time nor labor). In addition, some groups have brought their wages up and added health and other benefits, creating a laudable, though expensive, rise in their payment packages.

To deal with this increase in costs and the general financial insecurity that seems to pervade our nonprofit culture, grassroots groups now spend hours creating investment policies or deciding whether to buy board liability insurance. Some groups don't think they are fiscally sound unless they have a year's worth of funding lined up and six months' worth of operating costs in the bank. And more and more groups are creating endowments.

There is also the common trap of "raising money" by "saving" it — the opposite of increasing costs through infrastructure expenses and wage and benefit raises. Under pressure from their board to present a balanced budget and show a healthy reserve, executive directors will postpone projects, hirings, wage increases, printing jobs or anything else that will make the money go out more slowly. In the name of fiscal prudence, every expenditure is scrutinized and staff and board are constantly asked to "find someone to donate it." Organizations endure aged computers that cannot accommodate new software, office space that is dismal and depressing, and wages that are simply too low. In a recent study of benefits paid by nonprofits, only 71% had health insurance for their employees — a disgracefully low percentage.

Saving money does not necessarily equal fiscal prudence. In fact, in examining organizations with this mentality, we often find two kinds of staff — those who have been at the organization for many years, and those who come and go within 12 to 18 months. Those who have stayed seem noble and self-sacrificing until we look closer and discover that many have what a friend of mine calls a "financial fall-back position." These long-term staff either have a small inheritance, are married to someone who earns a decent salary, belong to a religious community that will provide for them in their retirement, or in some other way do not entirely depend on their income from their job in the nonprofit sector for their financial well-being. In organizations of this type, the pool of potential workers is narrowed to those who are starting out or those who have other sources of income.

There is an implicit assumption that with enough money you will feel secure, yet few groups ever feel secure no matter how much money they have. The quest for financial security, whether it takes the form of raising more and more money to be held in reserve, or spending less and less money till every dollar is squeezed to death, dampens creativity, enthusiasm and good work.

With all of this focus on finances, a discussion of a new project revolves less around whether it needs to be done because it is the mission of the group and will be successful than whether it will accrue funding to the group. These are obviously serious over-reactions to the fear of financial insecurity.

Finding a Balance

I am not against setting aside money in reserve or against creating endowments. I am in favor of saving money and getting maximum mileage from each dollar. And I applaud changing what you do to meet new needs or trying new approaches to old needs. What I am against is making decisions based on finances alone. Organizations should be mission-driven — every decision framed in terms of the mission and goals of the group. What the decision costs and where the money will come from then become logistical problems.

How does an organization, then, balance maintaining fiscal responsibility and long-term financial planning with a willingness to take risks? Most groups do not want to be like the abused women's shelter years ago, raising its rent money the night before it was due. Nor do they want to change their goals in response to fundraising opportunities. Like the individuals who run them, groups often start out with a huge capacity for risk but become more fiscally conservative over time.

The only way to avoid falling into the security trap is to make sure that all discussions of new programs and projects, salaries and benefits, and other decisions that have financial implications are approached with the caveat, "Let's pretend we have or can find the money." In a discussion held under this assumption, no one is allowed to criticize or modify an idea because it will cost too much, or "the money can't be raised." This freedom leaves room for good ideas to be fully developed.

Once the ideal scenario has been fleshed out and planned in some detail, then financial considerations can come in. These considerations will not nix the idea — they will simply provide a framework for it. "It will take two years to raise the money" is a very different way of thinking about an idea than, "How can we afford that right now?" Similarly, "We will have to find some new donors" has a different ring than, "Forget it. Our biggest donors will not go along with it."

It is also imperative for organizations to discuss what financial security and fiscal responsibility mean to them in light of their mission. There is a balance between not having the money to pay a debt until the night before it is due and having enough money in the bank to cover a year's worth of expenses. Each group will need to decide on that balance, and their decision may change as their programs change. For example, a group about to launch a capital campaign may want to have more money saved in case their annual fundraising declines while the capital campaign is in progress. A group with uncertain government funding will probably want more of a reserve than a group with a stable and growing base of individual donors.

Organizations need to think of other measurements of security besides money in the bank or in the pipeline. For example, if you have a solid, loyal base of donors, you can turn to them if you suddenly need money. Donors are really like an endowment — if your organization lets your donors know about the good work it is doing, if you thank them for their gifts and treat them as the partners in your work that they are, they will give a predictable amount of money every year and are likely to respond to a one-time need with further generosity. Donors yield money with more certainty and predictability than almost any investment.

Another option is to open a line of credit at your bank rather than maintain a large savings account. Groups that have done this create a policy that specifies both that the line of credit is only to be used in extreme circumstances and how the money borrowed will be paid back. This strategy provides a group a cash-flow infusion if desperately needed without requiring a large reserve fund.

When you look at your mission, you have to think about how you want to be remembered. "The group that had a reserve fund" is not catchy. Boldness has a life and power of its own. It is attractive and it attracts money. Ironically, the greatest financial security will be found in discarding financial security as a way to test an idea and measuring each proposal instead against the mission and goals of the organization. Donors pay you to do your work, not to exist in perpetuity. If you do something that some donors don't like, others will like you better for it and step in to take their place.

Stop asking, "Can we afford it?" and start every meeting instead with Ché Guevara's words, "Be realistic. Do the impossible."

Here are three case studies illustrating the security trap:

CASE STUDIES

Relinquishing the Reserve Fund

A free clinic with a year's worth of funding in reserve hired a new director. When she suggested using the reserve to open a satellite office in another neighborhood in need of a clinic, she met a great deal of resistance from several board members. Finally, one board member, who was also a clinic patient, confessed that she felt uncomfortable with the fact that the clinic had such a substantial reserve while its clients often didn't know where they would find the money for their next rent check. She felt that, as a result, a distance had grown up between the clinic and its clients. She proposed the board consider liquidating some of the reserve to start the satellite clinic and evaluate the real financial consequences of only having six months' worth of operating expenses set aside.

The board was persuaded and the satellite office not only opened, but generated a great deal of funding because of the services it provided. As a result, the board voted to maintain only between three and six months' worth of operating expenses in the bank. This has freed up a lot of money.

"We Make Our Nickels Scream"

When I was a child, the above expression was used to describe someone who was beyond frugal and thrifty, which were important values to my parents, and had crossed the line into cheap and penurious. I never thought I would hear this expression outside of my family, and I certainly never dreamed I would hear it expressed as a compliment. But I did when I was asked to consult with a hotline serving the gay/lesbian/bi-sexual/transgender (GLBT) community of a small town and its surrounding rural area. The area was very conservative, with a number or churches that had spoken out strongly against homosexuality and a mayor who had been quoted in the paper as saying, "These so-called 'gay' people can take their sick lifestyle to San Francisco and leave this town alone." Yet, there were some openly gay people, a gay bar, and this hotline in town. The hotline was staffed by volunteers 24 hours a day. About half of the callers were 20 years old or younger, terrified of coming out to their parents or their friends. Other callers sought information about their rights as tenants or workers or parents, and some just wanted to talk. Some days there would be a handful of calls, and some days there would be upwards of 100. Most days, there were about 25 calls, and in a year there were generally 10,000 calls. The hotline was seven years old. A retired businessman named Rodney served as the director and only paid staff. He had owned a small drugstore and sold it to a chain, so was able to work for a token salary. The budget of this group was $10,000 a year. I was called in because Rodney and some of the long-time volunteers were locked in a confrontation with the younger volunteers on issues of expanding the program, which would involve spending money. Their board, which would make the final decision, was composed of 14 hotline volunteers and the director as a tie-breaker. I was to help mediate this confrontation.

Each side's position was easy to understand. The hotline had no answering machine or voice mail system because it was staffed all the time. They did not have "call waiting" because they didn't want to interrupt a caller and so, from time to time, they heard from people that someone couldn't get through because both lines were busy. Although they served a large rural area, and were only one of two hotlines in their state, they did not have a toll-free number. People could call collect, but that was not advertised because they didn't want to incur that cost. It was hard to raise money for the hotline. They had two special events at the bar and board members gave money and asked their friends to give, but the anti-gay climate discouraged any public efforts to raise money. They had a small mailing list of people whom they approached once a year.

"We are volunteer-driven," Rodney explained to me proudly. "We squeeze every nickel until it screams. I like to think that we spend money as a last resort — when we don't have a choice, like our phone bill, or when we can't get something for free, like our rent. People bring their own pens and pencils from home. They bring their own snacks for meetings. We got our refrigerator and computer donated and we get our printing donated. We don't need much money to do our work, and so we don't have to spend a lot of time raising money. That's how we keep this hotline staffed 24/7."

The younger board members had a different view, presented by Tom. "We need a toll-free number so that people can call easily, especially teenagers. Teenagers don't want this number showing up on their parents' phone bill, and they may not be able to afford to call from a pay phone. A lot of people don't know they can call collect and they may not even know how to do that. Plus, we need a voice mail system so that when both lines are busy, people can leave a message. It may not happen that often, but when it does, it is usually because there is some crisis in the community and a lot of people want to talk about it." He then presented a proposal for a voice mail service that would cost $10 a month and a toll-free number that would cost $.10 a minute and have no monthly charge. He projected that, at first, few calls would come in on the toll-free line, but that within a year half of the calls would come in on the toll-free number. Currently, calls lasted an average of seven minutes. The cost of the toll-free line would be $200 a month to start and, as word spread, would go up to about $600 a month. The total budget increase he proposed was $4,900 for the first year and $7,300 for the following year. After two years, the group would have a better sense of the expense associated with the toll-free number. "I believe we can get that much by writing to our mailing list twice a year and asking a few major donors for more money," Tom suggested.

Marilyn, a volunteer with the hotline from its start, responded. "It is probably true that sometimes people cannot get through, but that is rare. It is way more common that we have one call in an hour and the other phone isn't ringing. There are only 70,000 people in this half of the state, so at most 7,000 are GLBT and they are not all in crisis. It doesn't seem like our lack of a toll-free number is keeping young people from calling — that is mostly who calls. We have a system that works fine. Your proposal almost doubles our budget, with no end in sight in increased cost with this toll-free number. I say no."

I told the group that I thought we could arrive at a conclusion that satisfied both sides, if each side was willing to change some of their paradigms. "You are getting 10,000 calls a year and your budget is $10,000, so each call costs $1.00. If you divide the $10,000 budget by 7,000 GLBT people, you are available 24 hours a day, 365 days a year for $1.42 per person per year in your area. You are also called by people who aren't gay — parents, ministers, friends. If we add those people into the total of your community, you become the cheapest date in town!" Both sides beamed proudly.

I went on to explain that like the old gambling song, "You've got to know when to hold 'em, know when to fold 'em..." groups had to know when it was appropriate to save money and when it was more appropriate to raise money that could be spent. This hotline had saving money down to a science. Now they had to think about spending money. "What if we can come up with a plan that involves very little more fundraising work on your parts and is able to raise the money needed? Are you willing to adopt the proposal presented by Tom?" I asked this question to surface if there were any other objections to Tom's plan besides the money it cost. There were not. Marilyn said she would pay the entire cost of the voice mail system for two years in addition to her regular gift. This allowed us to focus all attention on the toll-free number, but more important, it demonstrated good faith on the part of those originally opposed to the plan, as she had led the opposition. Tom and another board member, moved by Marilyn's donation, said they would approach three people they knew for $500 each to get the toll-free number going, and proposed not getting the line until they had raised at least $1,000. The group agreed.

Then they decided to send a letter to their mailing list asking everyone to pay for as many calls as they could at an average of a dollar per call. They enclosed two copies of the letter and asked that everyone on the list send the second copy to a friend.

This group was able to raise $2,500 from their mailing and $1,200 from two donors. With this cushion, the group agreed to go ahead with the toll-free number. The owner of the gay bar suggested putting a can on the bar and asking people to dump their change into it. A sign on the can tells about the toll-free number and its cost of $.10 a minute. About $150 a month gets dropped into the can.

What has taken the long-time volunteers and Rodney by surprise is that their ability to raise money has more than kept up with their increased costs. All parties in this dispute have learned some valuable lessons. First, thriftiness is good, but it can be taken to an extreme. Second, proposals for increased costs must be grounded in research. And third, people will give more when they are asked for more if the cause makes sense. Rodney told me several months after my initial meeting with them, "Now we tell our nickels to invite their friends."

The Pitfalls of Being Donor-Driven

Gray County has about 250,000 people and three main industries: agriculture, tourism and a branch of the state university. Over the course of the past two years the county has been hit with one thing after another: record rainfall destroyed the harvest two years in a row, other financial problems caused the university to cut back on its faculty and staff by 10%, and a rash of burglaries, car jackings, and assaults on tourists, including the murder of two tourists during a bungled burglary, depressed tourism revenues by about 25%.

Hardest hit are the agricultural workers, whose unemployment rates skyrocket and who have no social safety net. Next are those in the service industry: waiters, cooks, housecleaners and others who lose their jobs as restaurants lay off workers, bed-and-breakfast inns close and hotels function at two-thirds of their normal occupancy. The university's cutbacks add to the hundreds of laid-off workers the county has no ability to absorb. Many people respond by moving away, but others don't want to or can't.

As in most counties, a food bank operates in the largest town. The food bank provides groceries to a few hundred people each week and helps organize food pantries in local churches, community centers and health clinics around the county with the goal that no one has to travel more than two miles to get food. The food bank's policy is to give anyone food who says they need it. This honor system was important to the founders. One of the original board members says, "If people say they are hungry, we believe them. If they are in a grocery store, there is an assumption that they will pay for the food. If they are in line here, there is an assumption they will not. We don't ask any questions. Who these people are and how they got into this situation is not our business."

The food bank is well established by the time the county's financial crises hit, but it is quickly swamped by the number of people lining up for food. The numbers double, then triple, then quadruple. Their fundraising increases, but cannot keep up with the demand.

The food bank's director approaches the local archbishop for an emergency grant. The archbishop offers $10,000, with one condition: one of the food pantries in a very small town is located at a health center that provides birth control and referrals for abortions. The food bank must either move that food pantry or close it. The director consults with the chair of the board, who, feeling pressed for the money, agrees this pantry should be closed. The director hopes eventually to find another location. Meanwhile, he rationalizes, people in that area will only have to travel four miles to the next nearest food pantry. The $10,000 will tide the food bank over for three or four months.

A few weeks later the town newspaper, which is politically conservative, does a series of articles on social service nonprofits. A reporter comes to the food bank and asks if he can take pictures. The food bank's policy limits such photography to staff, the facility, food deliveries and so on; it prohibits pictures of people receiving food. But the reporter is doing a story called "The Face of Disaster," and he would like to photograph some of the recipients. The director consents on the condition that anyone to be photographed gives their permission. The reporter complies. In the published article the reporter notes that some people did not wish to be photographed because they were undocumented workers. Further, he reports that there were many able-bodied young people in line and he questions their need for free food. Other articles in the series raise similar questions about who the county's social service nonprofits are serving.

Some of the social service nonprofits fight back with opinion pieces, editorials, and letters to the editor criticizing the bias of this series of reports. The food bank director, again in consultation with the chair of the board, does not join the protests. The chair says they will blow over and there is no point in calling more attention to already negative publicity. Two of the food bank's founders, who are no longer on the board, ask the director to write a letter to the editor or give some kind of response, but he explains his position and they agree to wait and see what happens.

After these articles have appeared, the director is contacted by one of his biggest donors who asks how many "aliens" are being fed; the donor says he doesn't like his money going to "those kind of people." A few other donors call with similar concerns. They all want the food bank to begin screening food recipients. One threatens to withdraw his gift if this isn't done and the others imply that their gifts are being reconsidered. The director calls a meeting of the board's executive committee and the development director. He says he is being pushed too far. He has already caved in to the archbishop, but doesn't know what to do about these other donors and this bad publicity. The development director suggests a compromise. "The sign on our door says 'Serving the people of Gray County.' Let's change it to 'serving the citizens of Gray County' and tell these donors we are doing our best to sort out non-citizens." The sign is changed. The donors who complained about serving undocumented people seem placated because they continue to give.

The sign does not go unnoticed by the migrant workers, however, and many stop coming to the food bank even though they still need food. Several ministers in liberal churches with food pantries object to the sign and threaten to withdraw from the food bank and form their own food distribution network. The people at the health clinic are also upset because people are still coming to them for food and the director has not yet found an alternative location.

In the meantime, fundraising is up and the archbishop gives another $10,000. Again, the counsel of the board is not to engage in any direct confrontation either with the town's conservative forces or those inside the food distribution network.

Several new people join the board who have corporate connections. They know none of the history of the food bank and are not told of its original commitments to serve everyone without judgment or question within two miles of their home. One board member who is also a banker recruits five banks to give $5,000 each to the food bank. The banks hold a large press event and unfurl a sign saying, "Gray County Banks helping people who can't help themselves." That day, a news photographer takes pictures of the people in line for food without asking for permission.

The director winces at the sign and the photographer, but doesn't want to interrupt the press event. After all, he thinks, $25,000 is a lot of money.

For others, this is the last straw. The two ministers, two board members from the health clinic that lost their pantry and two of the founding board members of the food bank start their own group, "Gray County Action Against Hunger." It is an advocacy group, holding community forums and rallies about the root causes of hunger in America. It also reopens the pantry at the health clinic and opens food pantries in the migrant worker camps. The two groups co-exist and do not duplicate each other's work.

six

The Truth About Boards (and Fundraising)

I once had a bad dream in which I was giving a lecture on fundraising to an enormous crowd of people in a large lecture hall. In my dream I felt frightened, although I wasn't sure of what. I took a deep breath and said, "Boards don't work." I was booed and hissed at, and tomatoes were thrown at me. Then I woke up.

I probably won't say this in a lecture hall, but from the relative safety of the distance between you and me, I will say it here: generally, boards don't work.

Let me elaborate.

For almost 25 years, I have been teaching fundraising, consulting with organizations, working as a development person and serving on boards of directors. In that time, I have taught people from upwards of 5,000 groups, consulted individually with more than 500 groups, worked as a development director or person in charge of fundraising in five organizations and served on a dozen boards. Out of all those organizations, I have seen about 50 boards that really worked, including only two boards that I have served on.

I have tried many methods of getting boards to work, and I have written widely on the subject. It never occurred to me to question the premise of a volunteer board bearing ultimate responsibility for a nonprofit organization. Then, recently, a young woman approached me after a training session I had conducted for board members and said, "I am sorry if this sounds impertinent, but do you really know any boards that work?" Being quick on my feet, I named a few and she wandered off, seemingly satisfied.

I hope that woman questioned the authority of my answer because I owe her a great debt for that question. I had never really thought about what it means that almost every board I see is not functioning properly, that the most common complaint about an organization — whether from board members, staff, or volunteers not on the board — is something about the board — its performance, composition, lack of involvement or over-involvement with program, or relationship to staff. I had thought that, in the same way that a doctor sees a disproportionate number of sick people, I was seeing boards that needed help and not seeing the thousands that were functioning well. However, I finally had to wonder if there isn't something wrong with the idea of a board of directors, rather than a particular problem with each individual organization.

Consider these facts:

Board members are volunteers. They usually squeeze their board time into already overcrowded schedules and are asked to take moral, legal and fiscal responsibility for an organization: to hire, evaluate, and if necessary, fire, the executive director; to approve programs and budgets; and to monitor expenses and income. Volunteers, on their volunteer time, supervise paid professionals.

This board structure can work well when the volunteers have a decent amount of time to do the job properly, either because they don't work full time, or they can do their board work as part of their paid work elsewhere or when most of the work of the organization is done by volunteers and the group has one part-time staff person. This structure also works when board members are clearly getting some direct benefit out of the work, making it worth their time and effort.

The board structure that we have today has evolved over the past several decades as a growing number of nonprofits have sought to meet a growing number of needs. No group ever sat down and said, "How shall nonprofits best govern themselves?" and came out of their meeting with a document that described a board of directors. However, the structure ceased to evolve significantly after the 1960s, which means that we are working with a structure that suited nonprofits of a very different era, and imperfectly even then. In the 1960s, '70s and into the early '80s, the government played a much larger role in funding nonprofits. Further, many more people lived in families that needed only one income, and so one spouse (usually the woman) could do volunteer work. There were far fewer nonprofits and it was far less expensive and complicated to run them. In the days when a nonprofit required only an office, a typewriter and a phone, it was not that hard to raise the money needed.

Now, few nonprofits can run without fax machines, computers and several phone lines. The staff of an organization today have to be computer literate and know at least a little about accounting and management in addition to what they need to know about the issue the organization is addressing. Professional staff come at a higher cost, and put more distance between staff and board in terms of common knowledge and experience.

Although much about running a nonprofit has changed in the last 20 years, the structure used to govern them has not. Small wonder that many groups have a hard time making this structure work.

Far from solving problems with boards, as I had thought all these years, I was collaborating with the idea that a board of directors is an appropriate structure, and thinking that each individual board just needed some coaching. I was fooled by the following facts: a) a few boards are very good; b) on most boards, some board members are very good and carry the work of the board; c) some staff people are pleased with their boards most of the time; and d) I am generally a good board member. I had tried over and over to help everyone be a "good" board member and to help every executive director work more easily with their board. In short, I had made a large part of my living helping solve individual board problems, and my successes kept me from realizing that although boards can work better with some conscious effort, the root problem is the structure itself.

I still get calls from exasperated executive directors who say, "Can you come and knock some sense into my board?" Or from board chairs or nominating committee people who say, "We can make this board work if we have some corporate types, or some investment people." Sometimes when I am invited to sit on a board, I am told, "I think with your help, we can whip this board into shape."

I'd like to give up the idea of knocking, whipping or making a board do anything, and move to two non-violent suggestions: 1) let's put our collective heads together and see what variations on this structure we can create, and 2) until we have a better way of running nonprofits, let's help each board member and staff person understand the structure of the board and work with it.

A QUICK REVIEW OF THE ROLE
OF NONPROFIT BOARDS IN THE USA

I am assuming that your group is incorporated as a nonprofit tax-exempt entity known by the IRS category 501(c)3, or is under the umbrella of another organization's 501(c)3 status. If your organization is a 501(c)4, a PAC (Political Action Committee), or a service club, some of what is said here will apply to you and some will not. If you have chosen not to apply for tax-exempt status (which is true for millions of all-volunteer organizations, or more informal block clubs and associations), or you are from a country other than the United States, then the laws I describe here will not apply to you. However, if your organization works for the public good (even if the public is as small your neighborhood) and is not set up to make a profit, the moral implications of what I say here apply to you, so you may wish to skim the legal parts and move to the end of this section.

When an organization receives nonprofit tax-exempt status from their state and from the federal government under the IRS category 501(c)3, it takes on a large fiscal responsibility in return for a large government subsidy. A 501(c)3 tax status entitles an organization to the following benefits:

• It can receive donations for which the donor can take a tax deduction.

• It is exempt from most taxes, including taxes on property used for a tax-exempt purpose, income in excess of expenses in a year, capital gains and, in some states, sales tax. It does have to pay payroll tax and to collect sales tax on products it sells regularly.

• It has access that a business or individual doesn't have to money from private foundations (which cannot fund groups that don't have this status); public foundations (which can give a certain percentage of funds to groups without tax-exempt status but tend not to); corporations (which also prefer to fund groups with nonprofit, tax-exempt status); and government programs.

• It receives substantially discounted bulk mail rates from the U.S. Postal Service.

All of these privileges have to do with money, specifically tax money. The government realizes that a nonprofit cannot be expected to survive in a for-profit, free-market economy without significant help. Decreasing or eliminating taxes is the best way government can help. The government calls this tax relief "foregone revenue." Some experts estimate that the government underwrites upwards of $50 billion in foregone revenue annually.

Most of us would argue that this is a good deal — in return for $50 billion, the nation gets nearly 1.1 million nonprofit groups engaged in everything from advocacy, protecting civil rights, community organizing, providing health care, conducting research and providing social services to running museums, theaters, schools, religious organizations, and much more.

In return for this subsidy, 501(c)3-designated organizations are to be good stewards of this subsidy, as well as of the money donated to them directly. Specifically, 501(c)3s are limited in what they can do or say about political campaigns or candidates; they cannot have paid shareholders; and they must follow all laws that apply to corporations: the workplace must be safe, they cannot discriminate in hiring and firing practices, and the like. In addition, they cannot pay "excessive" compensation to the staff and board members who serve as volunteers.

The dealings of a nonprofit are supposed to be fairly transparent: minutes of board meetings are public information, their tax-return form (called a PF 990) is available to the public, and in general the nonprofit operates so that there is nothing to hide.

Thus, it is accurate to think of 501(c)3 tax status as a "contract" between the group and the Internal Revenue Service. The people who are charged with overseeing the nonprofit — for making sure that it lives up to the contract — are the board members.

The Fiduciary Responsibilities of Being a Board Member

The government asks each board member to act like a "prudent person." In other words, you are not required to know everything about running a nonprofit, but you are required to use common sense in making decisions and to plan ahead. The "prudent person" standard is most obvious in issues of how money is handled. A prudent person, for example, will realize that any person may be tempted to steal money if it is easy to do so, and so makes sure that embezzling funds is not easy by requiring that at least two people are involved in every large financial transaction. Two signatures are required on checks, two people count cash after an event, one person opens the mail and codes the checks for a deposit and another person makes the deposit, and the like. A prudent person ensures that money is spent properly and accounted for through budgets, financial reports and, in larger organizations, audits. Failure to be prudent can result in fines, suspension or even revocation of tax status and, in extreme cases, financial liabilities that individual board members have to pay.

Most people learn about their responsibilities as board members the hard way. Certainly that is how I learned. When I served on my first board I was 24 years old, and flattered to be asked. The group was pioneering a creative approach to alcohol and drug addiction — the counselors had to be recovering addicts, with less than six months' sobriety. Their jobs would be temporary, and they would be replaced by people coming through the program. The idea was that the counselors were very close to the problems they were addressing and therefore of more help to the clients. The program was funded by a grant from the California Health Department.

The executive director was a charismatic recovering alcoholic. She said she had been sober off and on for 20 years, having never stayed sober for more than three years at a time. She said she understood failure and had deep empathy for people coming to the program. She understood recovery, and she was determined to stay sober. She was warm, funny, and hardworking. We thought she was perfect for the job. All five board members were serving on their first board and our oldest member was 25. We knew nothing about what to look for in a director or what the rest of our jobs as board members entailed. The director did well for about six months, then started being absent from work a lot. Finally, she left town altogether, with piles of unpaid bills, overdue reports and general chaos in her wake.

The state pulled its funding immediately and demanded an accounting of the money that had been spent. They sent an auditor, and while it appeared that none of the money had been embezzled, it had been misspent on office furniture, travel expenses, food for meetings and so on. The number of people helped by the program was very small.

The program was closed down and the state demanded part of its grant back. We sold all the assets the organization had and still owed $15,000. Much to my surprise, because the grant was government money, the state held the board members personally liable for the debt. However, because of our age and lack of assets, they settled for $5,000 and waived the interest. Each of the board members paid $1,000. Since I was only earning $6,000 that year, I had to take two years to pay my share. Looking back, I think of it as an inexpensive lesson in board responsibility.

Yet, in the thousands of trainings I have done, the majority of board members I have met have not understood the seriousness or the scope of their responsibility. By and large, they have not been told anything about what is expected of them except attendance at meetings. Often staff people are not aware of the extent of board liability, and because rarely are a nonprofit's board members held liable for imprudent decisions resulting in debts to the government, people sail through one board experience after another without knowing even the basics of what they have signed on to. All the details of a board's fiduciary responsibility and the punishments that can be meted out for failure to be good stewards can be found in various board handbooks. It is enough to note that most people don't know enough to be prudent board members.

Board Members and Fundraising

Although a board's participation in fundraising is not required by law, the implications of taking responsibility for the financial health of an organization are that board members must test on themselves the proposition that the group is worth supporting and make their own gift first, and they must help raise money.

It is in the arena of fundraising that I have found the least clarity among board members about their roles. In newer organizations, board members may not be aware that they are expected to help with fundraising; in older groups, while this expectation may be known, it usually has no structure attached to it, so what board members should be doing remains mysterious to them. This puzzle gives rise to the following types of frustrations for board members:

• They sense that whatever they do is not enough and that their reward for doing their work is more work.

- They work hard on a project and finish what they committed to do, only to find that few other people did the same.
- They suspect that decisions are made by a cabal that they are not part of.
- They notice that the staff resents them if they ask too many questions, particularly about budgeting or finance.
- They feel the only job expected of them is to raise money, often without a plan or guidance.

Many people go from board to board looking for a better experience, and finally give up altogether. There are thousands of these people: board dropouts who are bright, well intentioned and committed to some issue or other but who have had one too many demoralizing experiences. A friend of mine was reprimanded by an executive director for not being loyal when as a board member she questioned the organization's salary structure. She told me, "If I wanted to be talked to like that, I would visit my ex-husband."

Coming Clean

There is extensive and excellent writing, videotapes, and training on how to help board members understand their role. Obviously all board members should have orientation sessions, some kind of job description or statement of agreement, copies of by-laws, ways to evaluate themselves, and so on. The bibliography can guide readers to that information. A key question for our purposes is, Why don't groups tell prospective board members what is expected from them? This disclosure would allow people who really don't have the time or willingness to do the work required of a board member to decline the offer to be on the board. It would allow board members to hold each other accountable and possibly even to ask one of their number to leave.

A board member is like an unpaid staff member. No one thinks that a healthy staff position is one in which the person just makes up the job as she goes along, with no guidance and no evaluation. The logic of telling people what is expected of them is clear. The reason that board members are often not told what is expected of them is, at the most innocent end of the spectrum, the fact that no one in the group understands what can be expected of a board. At the most dysfunctional end of the spectrum, it is because the organization has no confidence that people would want to make the sacrifices it takes to do the work entailed.

I have heard dozens of staff and board members exclaim, "If we told the board what was expected of them, we would have only three board members left." What a group with that attitude has to face is that they have only three board members now, and the rest of the board members are taking up space to no purpose. They have been invited on the board because of a perception that they "have money," or they "have contacts" or "they can open doors." They are probably not told that is why they have been invited and they may not perceive themselves the way the group does. In fact, often board members are doing exactly what they were asked to do by whoever asked them to join the board. The board may have other expectations it doesn't set forth or doesn't realize are not clear. Clarity of expectation is key to the healthy functioning of any person who is part of a group, whether board, staff, family, classroom, or sports team.

A person should be asked to join a board for one overriding reason: because they care deeply about the work of the group. They should be passionately committed to the mission and goals of the organization. And they should have demonstrated that passion in some way — by volunteering for the group, by working in some capacity for a similar group, by donating significant amounts of money relative to their resources, and so on. People who have passion can learn to be board members. Their background, their education, their economic standing are utterly secondary to that commitment.

So, in order to have a working, functional board, you need to be clear about what the board is required to do and you need to find people who love the organization enough that they are willing to do whatever it takes to keep it going.

MAKING THE STRUCTURE WORK

Knowing what the job entails and being clear about it with a dedicated board will solve at least part of your problem. The other half of the problem will be solved by acknowledging that the structure of a board is problematic.

As many organizational development and board consultants have commented, a big part of the problem with board structure is the "one size fits all" nature of it. Many organizations try to squeeze themselves into a model that would work well for another kind of group, but does not suit them at all. Being willing to try variations on board structure, experiment with different ways of making decisions, dividing tasks, running meetings, or selecting board members will allow your group to find a structure that works. That structure will work until it doesn't.

As many organizational development experts have pointed out, a group is a living organism. Its needs change as the members of the group change. To have a workable structure for your group may mean changing parts of it or all of it from time to time.

The following are some variations on board structures for grassroots social justice nonprofits. While I have seen some of these work, I would like to see groups use and perfect them more. To get them to work for your group may require cutting and pasting, adopting all, then abandoning parts, or using these suggestions as launching pads for something brand new.

I believe we can think of something better if we get out of the idea that it will be one thing or that it will last for more than a decade. Further, these suggestions focus primarily on what works best to get a board to participate in fundraising. My experience is that boards that do their job with regard to fundraising generally do their other work very well.

ALTERNATIVE ONE: The Small Board

This alternative takes a common problem, which is that only a few people on the board actually work hard, and solves it by having that small group be the board. The board has three to five people on it. Those people meet with the director regularly. Quorums are not difficult to achieve, decisions are made by people familiar with the issues and not just dropping in occasionally for a meeting, and some work can be done by conference call or e-mail because so few people are involved. Many groups have this system in place in the form of an executive committee which does a huge amount of work and reports to the board, bringing large decisions to board meetings. While an executive committee can work well, it can also get bogged down in having to repeat discussions and revisit decisions at the board level.

A small board can be involved in fundraising, but works best with a number of ad hoc committees of people not on the board who come together for certain tasks, such as a special event, the major donor campaign or the membership drive.

To avoid become an insular elite, the five people must represent different constituencies in the organization, and two of the five should change every year. Each person should serve a three-year term, but terms should be staggered so that no one would serve all three years with more than one other person.

ALTERNATIVE TWO: Staff on Board

Just as I used to be a fan of big boards, I used to be adamantly opposed to paid staff being on the board. Having seen it work a number of times, I have modified my position. There are obvious problems with having paid staff on the board: they have to oversee work that they also implement; they have none of the distance from the work that is part of the reason for having a board (being able to see the forest, not just the trees), and they have a lot of power because they have the power of the staff combined with the power of a board member.

This structure also has a number of advantages. It blurs, and sometimes even erases, staff/board tension. Staff get to see the work of the organization from two critical viewpoints — their own and those of the board members. Further, it recognizes that staff carry out most of the work that the organization does and allows them an equal say in what that work is and how it is evaluated. In organizations where staff sit on the board, I have noticed that there is no hiding mistakes or figuring out how to tell the board something they may not be pleased to hear.

To work best, there should be two non-staff for every staff person on the board. The executive director should not be the only staff person on the board. Some would argue that the executive director is the one staff person that should never be on the board because it gives that person more power than anyone else in the group, since they supervise other staff and report to the board as their employer. I think each group will have to decide that. In groups that only have one or two staff, the director doesn't have that much power to aggrandize or abuse.

ALTERNATIVE THREE: Ad Hoc Committees

In this alternative, the board can be small or very large, but the work of the organization is done by a number of committees made up of board and non-board members, possibly including staff. Each committee has a lot of autonomy coupled with a clear sense of their boundaries and responsibilities. They come together to complete a task and then they dissolve into another committee. The full board meets no more often than quarterly to decide what committees will exist for the next period of time and who will be on them. Once a year, the board and staff, in a one- or two-day retreat, prepare an extensive work plan for the year. Generally, this structure calls for some kind of oversight committee, which would traditionally be the executive committee. These ad hoc committees should not be limited to the traditional committee names and functions, such as Nominating, Personnel, Finance and so on. You can have the Winter, Spring, Summer and Fall committees, with five to seven people taking full board responsibility for one quarter of the year. The rest of the board participates as needed. This works well for the very busy people we tend to attract to our boards — they will carve out the time for a short period but aren't able to sustain that level of commitment for a whole year.

This structure is ideal for fundraising because board members agree to work on some aspect of fundraising, and their reward for doing their work is that their work is over. The Major Donor Campaign Committee, for example, might work for 10 weeks preparing, carrying out and evaluating a major gift drive, and then the people on that committee would not have to think about fundraising again until the next major donor drive or until they volunteered for some other aspect of fundraising.

For maximum effectiveness, one paid staff person will need to devote about half of their time to staffing these committees so that they do their work and don't spin out of control.

THE BASICS FOR ANY WORKABLE STRUCTURE

To get any structure to work for fundraising will require implementing the very pedestrian suggestions below. Like vacuuming, showering, or driving, there are certain motions one has to go through and they will be the same regardless of the make or model of your vacuum, shower or car.

Here is what you can do to have a board that works:

1. Choose board members with the same care you use in choosing staff. Board members are simply unpaid staff. When you hire staff, unless the perfect person presents themselves, you advertise, you read resumes, you interview and you choose from a pool. Do as much for your board members. Draw up a job description. Put an announcement in your newsletter and send it around to people who might know others who would be good board members. Ask people to apply to be on the board and develop a simple application form. If someone won't take the time to fill out an application, then how much time will they have for the board position?

Just as staff are sometimes promoted to a new position, volunteers and committee members who have shown themselves to be reliable, thoughtful and who work well in a group can be promoted to a board position.

2. Institute an evaluation process. The board should evaluate itself every year. What are they doing well? What could be improved? As with any evaluation, this should be done in the spirit of seeing problems as opportunities for change and growth. Every person and every board has problems. The problems don't have to be terminal, and generally they can be solved, or at least changed into less serious problems.

3. Maintain flexibility, but don't confuse this with having double standards. What often kills the teamwork of a board is considering one or two people so important to the group that they are excused from raising money or coming to meetings. If you have some people who are very important to your cause, but who don't want to do all the work of a board member, put them on an advisory council of some kind.

4. Agree on how the meetings are run. If you have 17 board members, you will have at least 17 opinions about how meetings should be run. One person has learned Robert's Rules of Order and is a stickler for that system. Someone else prefers a more casual approach where everyone shouts out their opinions. Some people get up and move around or get coffee during discussions, which other people interpret as not paying attention. The chair of the board, or whoever is the facilitator, needs to learn how to facilitate meetings. Most people know that running a meeting is a skill. What is less obvious is that being in a meeting is also a skill. Both are skills that can be learned. A fun in-service for a board meeting is a 30-minute presentation on how to make meetings work. Then the board members can choose what style they want to follow and establish the rules of their meetings.

The more casual the meeting style, the less likely shy people are to speak. I recommend having a more formal style in which people raise their hands and wait to be called on. Groups work best for people who feel confident talking in front of a group, and a facilitator has to make sure that all the members are given a way to voice their opinions, particularly board members who have significant differences in education, age, language or culture. Occasionally, the facilitator should ask that everyone speak on the subject under discussion. Often the chair will need to pause while slowly counting to 10 after asking, "Does anyone else have something to say on this subject?"

5. Make sure everyone knows ahead of time what will be covered at the meeting and has the chance to come prepared to discuss each item. It is helpful to have a blackboard or an easel with paper and marking pens for help with discussion of complicated items. Then everyone is looking at and responding to the same information. Many people need to see something in writing before they can really understand it. While having written materials is important, simply relying on people looking at their own copy of the fundraising plan or the budget will mean that people will shuffle through their papers, and if they can't find the item or find it but can't understand it, they may be tempted to act as though they know what is going on.

6. Give board members a number of ways to be involved in fundraising. Since fundraising is the main place that board work breaks down, even in otherwise high functioning boards, it is important to pay special attention to this responsibility. People need a range of choices with regard to fundraising, but also must understand that doing nothing to help raise money is not one of the choices. The sidebar suggests 10 ways board members can help with fundraising that do not require them asking for money in person or on the phone.

7. Use board members' time wisely. Even for the most dedicated board member, service on the board is a lower priority than many other things in life. Their family or friends come first, followed by their job, and then by what it takes to maintain one's life, such as laundry, grocery shopping, cleaning house, driving kids to activities and so on. For many people, there is not enough time even to fulfill those priorities, let alone add the six or eight hours a month necessary to be a board member. If most of that time is spent in meetings, there is little time left to do the work they committed to during the meetings. Cutting down meeting time will free up board members' time to do other board work.

8. Structure in detail the work you want from board members. If you want them to send in names of friends who should be invited to a special event, send them a form to fill out and a return envelope, or ask them to bring their address books to a board meeting and take some time to fill out forms there. Every task should be clear and have a deadline. The deadline should not be very long after the task is agreed to. Most people do a task right before it is due, so giving them a long time to accomplish it only postpones the results. The more specific you are, the more likely it is that the task will get done and get done right.

9. Make being on the board interesting and occasionally fun. Make sure board members are as involved in developing the program of the organization as they are in fundraising, managing personnel and revising by-laws. Board meetings are too often seen by the board as boring and by the staff as a burdensome requirement of the law. There is no reason for this. If the mission and programs of your organization are important and interesting, then any gathering of people committed to them should be important and interesting also. They should be used as a time to go deeper into organizational issues, think bigger in terms of program and money, and get re-charged for the job of being an ambassador of the organization to friends and colleagues.

Ten Ways Board Members Can Help Raise Money without Asking for It Out Loud

- - - - - - - - - - - - - - - - -

1. Write thank-you notes. Board members can thank not only donors, but also volunteers, vendors who reduce their prices for the group, foundation funders and anyone who has gone out of their way for the group.

2. Work on special events, from planning and all the work that has to be done beforehand, through set-up and clean-up.

3. Computer-literate board members can help enter data about donors into the computer database, or update the group's Web site and link it to those of other groups.

4. Conduct research about potential donors — foundations, corporations, or individuals.

5. Proofread fundraising letters, reports, newsletters and so on.

6. Write, edit or design fundraising letters, reports, newsletters and so on.

7. Make a list of friends who might be interested in the organization. Add their names to the next direct mail appeal, or better, write them a personal solicitation letter.

8. Collect other lists of people who might be interested in the group and send them a direct mail appeal. These lists might be people they go to religious services with, members of their block association, or members of other groups they belong to. They should be sure they have permission to use the list, and, from time to time, offer to share the organization's list.

9. Screen the mail. Read the newsletters, journals, reports and other fundraising information that comes through every development office and throw away what isn't useful, compile what is and summarize long reports into short paragraphs.

10. Help evaluate how well the group is doing on its annual plan, including looking at budgets, cash flow, cost/benefit, and income projections over several years.

In the end, for a board to function well it must view itself, and be seen by the staff, as a group of people who care deeply about the goals of the organization and are willing to give some of their most precious non-renewable resource — their time — to furthering these goals. A board that works is a board always in process and always looking at what it is doing well and what needs improving.

seven

When Fundraising Strategies Wear Out

Nearly all organizations have three fundraising fantasies:

Fantasy One: The Council on Foundations declares their group, "The group to fund now and forever" and, using one simple proposal photocopied over and over, the organization applies to several foundations and receives lots of money. Because no strings are attached to this money, there will be few reporting requirements.

Fantasy Two: Someone whom no one in the organization knows dies and leaves the group $1,000,000 to do with as they see fit. Because no one knew the person, no one in the group is bereft at their loss.

Fantasy Three (when it is clear the other two aren't happening): The organization creates a perfect fundraising plan in which all the strategies work well and there are plenty of volunteers to help with the work. Although fundraising takes some time, no one resents doing it because the strategies are lucrative and fun. Every year the group uses the same plan and makes more money.

Fantasy Three has a lot going for it. It is based in some reality. It calls for a plan, recognizes that fundraising takes time, and acknowledges that you have to fundraise every year. In fact, Fantasy Three only goes wrong when it postulates that one plan will be created and used successfully year after year.

WEAR AND TEAR

Like anything else, fundraising strategies wear out. Like taking care of a car, the trick is to anticipate wear and tear and deal with it before damage is done. There are a number of reasons that fundraising strategies get stale. Most common is that people in the organization get tired of them and start taking shortcuts. Mail appeals get terse and boring. The newsletter is full of typos and the articles lack passion. Thank-you notes are photocopied, with the donor's name filled in by a volunteer.

The second most common reason is that a strategy that works well for one or two groups is adopted by many groups and thus its effectiveness is decreased for everyone. This situation is particularly true with special events. One group has a successful dance-a-thon. They get a lot of publicity and everyone has a great time. So another group does a dance-a-thon. They do well. After the third or fourth or fifth group does one, people get tired of dance-a-thons and look around for something new to do. The dance-a-thon as a fundraising strategy starts to be less effective.

The same fate can befall almost any strategy. Even major donor campaigns (my personal favorite) lose some of their original effectiveness when they are over-used in a small community and many groups approach the same donors.

Finally, there is the problem of market saturation. Direct mail, phone solicitation and other mass appeal strategies are now alienating almost as many donors as they attract. It is hard to keep a feeling of excitement about your appeal letter if you know that it will show up next to 20 other worthy appeal letters in a donor's mailbox.

All of these causes of worn-out strategies are related to each other. It is hard not to get cynical about these problems when the struggle to raise enough money is never ending, and even if you succeed in raising the amount of money you need for one year you will only have to start over the next.

HOW TO PREVENT A STRATEGY FROM WEARING OUT

Here are three things you can do to keep your fundraising strategies fresh:

1. *Let different people in the organization take the lead on fundraising strategies.* For example, no one person should write all the mail appeals. Ask board members or volunteers to write a first draft. Get someone who has benefited from your work to write a testimonial. The fundraising staff can then work with these letters, but they will have a new tone and a different approach from what you would have come up with.

Ditto for editing the newsletter. While one person should probably oversee and make final decisions about content, it is deadly for one person always to be in charge of the writing.

Double ditto for thank-you notes. The minute you stop adding personal notes to your thank-you notes, get someone else in there to help you. Volunteers and board members usually don't mind writing thank-you notes (particularly when this fills some of their fundraising obligations), and a personal note is infinitely better than a form letter.

2. *Try variations on a theme.* Suppose your community has a dozen awards dinners, or that people are often invited to house parties. If those are common strategies in your

area, then send a mail appeal for a "phantom event" inviting people to stay home. Tell your invitees that they have won an award from your group — the award is that they can put their feet up and have a nice cup of tea, right after they write your group a check. They don't need to go anywhere or listen to a fundraising pitch — they just send the cash and relax at home. (Some groups even include a tea bag in the mailing.)

3. Don't discard a strategy too soon. Remember that just because you are tired of a strategy, it doesn't mean the donor is. I have a favorite Italian restaurant. I don't care if the people who work there get tired of fixing Italian food. I want Italian food when I go there. I want the same menu and the same decor. The same is true of my favorite vacation spots — I keep going back because I know what they offer and I like it. Don't project onto the donor your own lack of enthusiasm for the strategy.

NOTHING WORKS FOREVER

Even so, strategies do wear out. For example, a phantom event will work for one or two years, or every other year, but eventually it will become "another non-event appeal" to be thrown in the wastebasket. This is especially true when the same groups that took on your dance-a-thon idea are now copying your phantom event.

A fundraising event takes at least one year to get going, but often wears itself out after seven or eight years. Similarly, predictable quarterly mail appeals need to be spruced up and varied in terms of timing, theme, design and such, or they too will begin to get tossed after a few years.

So, how can you tell if it is you who are tired or the donor? How do you know if the strategy needs a little remodeling or should be junked altogether? The answer is that often you don't know. You make your best guess. You can ask other people what they think and take that into account, but they may be reacting from their own tiredness unrelated to your event or campaign.

Here are three examples for guidance:

The Community Center Friendraiser

A community center in a rural area did a movie benefit every year, based on an old popular film. Before showing the movie, the group put on a short play that was a satire adapting the story line of the movie to their town. For several years this event got more and more popular. The plays were as well received as the movie and were often really hilarious. Modifying movies like "Singing in the Rain," "Casablanca" or "The Ten Commandments" to take place in their community was fun for the writers and actors, so it wasn't difficult to get people to participate.

But over time a number of problems developed. First, to keep the event available to the whole community, the ticket prices were low. As a result, it didn't generate a lot of money; even with sales of popcorn and soda the profit was not great. Second, the plays were sometimes too long and the jokes were sometimes too obscure for the audience. Third, after five or six years it got hard to keep finding movies that could be made into an entertaining play and the novelty of the event began to wear off. Attendance began to fall after the fourth year and was eventually reduced to pretty much the same people who also supported the group by mail.

When the development director called everyone together to begin the planning process for the seventh annual show, she hoped she could stimulate some excitement if she provoked her volunteers into defending the event. So she started by saying, "Let's not do this event again. It's getting boring." Much to her surprise, several volunteers agreed with her. "Let's quit while we are ahead," said one. "I agree," said another. "Let's stop now and wait for people to beg us to do this event again." "Much better than having them beg us not to do it," said a third. Others only disagreed half-heartedly. "What else are we going to do?" they said. Since they didn't have an idea of how to replace the movie event, they hired me to help them figure out where to go from there.

We worked together in one long meeting. They had taken the most important step which was to admit there was a problem. The first question I asked was, "Whose problem is it? Are the organizers worn out, but the audience happy or is everyone pretty much out of steam on this one?" Their answer came fairly easily: both organizers and audience were tired of this event.

Before deciding what to do about it, they enumerated their three goals for holding an event:

1. Bring the whole community together for a fun time. This means the event has to be affordable and children need to be welcome and entertained.

2. Bring in people who have not come to the community center before, in particular newcomers as the rural town expands and the people who work on the surrounding farms who generally don't come to events.

3. Make more money than the film/play event had brought in. The group agreed that in their efforts to be affordable they had "given away the store." They would have to create some income-generation methods as part of the event to boost revenues.

All three of these goals are appropriate to special events. In this instance, I pointed out that a compromise may need to be made between making more money from the event and bringing the whole community together. An event that is affordable for a range of people is not going to be a major money-maker. After more discussion, this is the event idea the group came up with:

1. Discard the old movie idea.

2. Turn the event into a talent show. Since what attracted the most people to the movie night was creating the play, this would be a natural successor and give more people a chance to get on stage. Each act would be given a time limit and people wanting to be in the show would apply by describing their talent and paying a nominal fee to participate.

3. Add a community fair component to increase income, encouraging merchants, craftspeople and restaurants to have booths in the lobby of the community center where people could shop and eat before the performance. Fees for the booths would be competitive with those at other fairs and events and would generate the additional money the group wants to raise.

4. Create a small adbook containing the program for the talent show. The many self-employed people in the community could advertise their plumbing, contracting, massage, art therapy, tarot reading and other talents for enough money to cover the cost of producing the adbook itself and generate a little profit.

5. Be thinking of the next variation. See this talent show idea as lasting about three or four years and evolving into something else. It has the seeds of a number of other events: a crafts show, a showcase for outside professional talent, a food fair, and so on.

The first talent show was held on a Saturday afternoon. Many people from the outlying farms who came into town for supplies stayed for the event or browsed at the booths. The event had a lot more foot traffic because people could come to see the booths without attending the talent show or they could just stay for part of the show. Admission to the talent show was only $2 and was free for children.

The community turned out a lot of talent and it was clear that the talent show idea will work for quite a while. Some people were disappointed that there was no movie, so next year they may add a movie as evening entertainment.

At its most successful, the old movie/play event had 200 people in the audience and netted about $2,000. With the income from the booths, the adbook and the entry fees for the talent show, the new event netted $5,000 from about 300 people attending in its first year.

The event is still a lot of work, but the income and the new audience and participants have created a new event that will serve the community center for some time.

Fine-Tuning the Phone-a-Thon

An environmental group has done a phone-a-thon every year. Board members and volunteers call all the group's members to ask them to renew their membership and take some action on an issue, such as writing a letter or calling a legislator. The callers also answer any questions members raise about the group's work.

The group started using this strategy five years ago when they had about 200 members and were working on a high-profile and fairly complicated worker health-and-safety issue. They have now grown to 1,000 members and have a number of different programs, which they discuss in detail in their newsletter.

Calling all 1,000 donors has made the phone-a-thon onerous. It now extends over several nights. Because many of the members are enthusiastic supporters, they ask a lot of questions about the group's work and what it thinks about various environmental issues. Although this enthusiasm is positive, the phone-a-thon takes a lot of time, as does training the volunteer callers.

The board and staff of the organization resist going to an entirely mail-based membership renewal system for two reasons. First, some find the phone-a-thon effective and enjoyable in renewing the relationships they have established with many of these donors over the years. Second, they feel that phoning is a more environmental strategy than writing.

However, the development director sees several problems. It is difficult to find enough volunteers to make all the calls; getting phone numbers for each member as they join is not always possible; and it takes two to three calls to reach most people, which is frustrating and time-consuming for the callers. Overall, she feels the amount of time the process takes is not justified by the returns.

In considering what to do, the group recalls that the original goal of the phone-a-thon — to build a strong membership base with people who could be counted on to be politically active on the issues as well as give money — is no longer valid. While 200 of the members might still carry out political actions, keeping 1,000 people mobilized takes much more staff than this group has. The group restates as the primary goal of this strategy raising money from the members. Knowing this, they are able to solve their problem.

They decide to segment their donors into three categories. The first category contains people who give less than $100, who have responded well in the past to being called, and/or whom the board and volunteers who will be doing the phone-a-thon know personally. These are the people who will be called during the phone-a-thon. The second category is made up of people who have given at least $100 for more than three years in a row. These people will be moved into a major gifts campaign. Instead of being called during the phone-a-thon, they will be called at another time by someone from a major gifts committee and offered the opportunity to meet personally with someone from the group. At that meeting they will be solicited for an increased donation. The last category encompasses everyone else on the list. This group — by far the largest — will be sent a renewal letter. Just in case some of these people really did look forward to their annual phone contact, the letter will say, "If you would like to talk to one of our volunteers, do not send back your membership dues now. Just wait for our call. If you would rather not be disturbed, or you are not going to be in on the nights of our phone-a-thon, please send in your membership today." Many of those who do not send back their renewals are probably not going to renew. Those who are not home when called will be sent a second letter asking them to renew. If they do not respond, they will be put into a lapsed file. Once a year the people in this file will be sent an appeal asking them to re-join. Those who don't respond to that appeal will be deleted from the database altogether.

Sorting the names, getting volunteers to go through the names, and then getting a letter out takes the same amount of work for the development director as organizing the phone-a-thon used to. However, the organization is now doing a mail appeal, a personalized phone appeal to the most likely responders, and they are ready for their major gifts campaign. They are now using the phone-a-thon properly and working with the donors properly.

A Sustainable Sustainer Program

The final example looks at a group that makes even more radical changes to their strategy. This organization publishes a magazine that goes to about 6,000 subscribers. The income from the subscriptions does not cover the cost of the magazine, so the group decides to institute a "sustainer" program, asking people to give money over and above their subscription fee.

They hire someone with a strong marketing background to develop the program and, over two years, this person puts in place an elaborate, tiered sustainer system. The basic magazine subscription is $15. For $35, subscribers also get a T-shirt. For $100, they get the T-shirt and a poster. For $250, they get the T-shirt, poster and a book written by an author the magazine features. For $500 or more they get all these benefits plus an invitation to a reception for a celebrity.

For three years the group raises a lot of money with this program. Even factoring in the staff time needed to send all the benefits, they show a handsome profit. But after three years their retention rate starts to fall. Many people who had given $35 drop back to $15. It takes work to have a new T-shirt designed every year and to find a new book. Staff begin to grouse about the time the fulfillment takes and the marketing person is offered a higher-paying job at a commercial magazine and leaves.

The executive director and board change the marketing job description to a development position and hire someone who has both marketing and fundraising experience. This person makes a small change at first. In the reply device, she adds a box for the sustainer to check if they do not want the benefit for their gift, or if they would like it sent to someone else.

When more than half of the sustainers check that they do not want the benefit and about one-third of the others either have their benefit sent to someone else or say, "Send it to someone who wants it," the development director knows what to do about this cumbersome program. She gets rid of it altogether, all at once.

Loud cries are heard from staff (those who were grousing previously) that "You can't just cut things off like that," but not a peep is heard from the sustainers. At the end of two more years, her sustainer renewal rate is slightly lower than her predecessor's, but without the cost of the benefits and the time fulfilling them, the income is much higher. People are simply asked to give $35, $50, $100 or whatever they can afford. Those who give $100 or more are called and, if they are willing, are visited and asked for an even higher gift.

Through this process, the development director has more than doubled the number of people giving $500–$1,000 from 10 to 25, and increased the number giving $250–$499 from 30 to 100. From time to time, when a book is published by someone who writes for the magazine, she makes it available to sustainers for a fraction of its retail price.

In this way, the organization has gotten rid of those donors who were actually shoppers disguised as donors and has built a strong base of people loyal to the magazine, not the benefits.

KEEP SIGHT OF THE GOAL

Fundraising strategies should be examined every year to make sure they are doing what they are supposed to do in terms of your overall fundraising plan. Just because something has worked in the past doesn't mean it will always work. Your strategies will have to be modified, revamped and sometimes scrapped to meet the needs of a growing organization.

On the other hand, if something isn't working up to par, it could possibly be made to work with a few adjustments. Keep your eyes on the overall goal. Be detached from the details, and don't take it personally if the thing that needs to change is your favorite strategy.

eight

Taking Donors for Granted

When I was first working at the Coalition for the Medical Rights of Women in San Francisco in 1978, donor files were kept in a card catalog. There was a card for each donor containing his or her name, address, phone number and history of giving. That was our database, since no nonprofit had computers then. I loved looking through those cards, seeing the names of people who had given for two years, three years, or even from the beginning, four years earlier. Some enthusiastic people gave two or three times a year! We were a membership organization, and the first few times I sent out renewal letters I was thrilled when people sent back money. I often included personal notes on my thank you notes, especially to major donors.

Over time, two things happened. One is that I got busier. The organization was growing and I was coordinating raising more and more money. The second is that the thrill of getting these donations wore off. I sent out the letters and the money came back. Some of my renewal letters were well written and some were not, yet the members sent their money. They were very loyal and I began to take them for granted.

Sometimes thank-you notes would be sent quite late. Once, I photocopied a form thank-you letter and sent that out. It came out crooked and slightly smeared, but I did not do it over because I didn't have time. (We used a photocopy machine at an office supply store down the street, so photocopying was time consuming and expensive.) While I never got any negative feedback, I distinctly remember running into a member and telling her how busy we were and how much was happening. She was pleased with our progress but said wistfully as we concluded our conversation, "I miss your personal notes. I always felt so appreciated by you." She continued to give, but her remark stayed with me.

Since then, I have seen this phenomenon a lot. Because donors don't give us very much feedback, we don't know what they notice and what they don't. If a name is spelled wrong, or left out of an Annual Report, or a person is sent duplicate copies

111

of an appeal, we will probably hear about it with varying degrees of irritation. However, few people will call to say, "Thanks for the personal note," or "Thanks for the phone call reminding me about the event." Under the pressures of time, we abandon the smaller gestures of appreciation and we don't really know what that costs our organizations.

This lack of attention to donors takes on bigger forms, however, where costs can be measured. For example, as organizations grow, they often cease to pay attention to patterns in their donors' giving. This is often compounded by the limitations of the database. For example, a donor sends in $35 to renew his membership and is thanked with a form letter. That same donor sends in an additional $35 using the return envelope in the newsletter, and later gives $35 in response to an appeal. Every time, he is thanked with the same form letter. No one is paying attention to the fact that his cumulative giving is becoming substantial. Ideally, after the second or third gift, he would receive a personal thank-you note that said, "Thanks for helping us so often — it means a lot." Further, he should come to the attention of the major donor committee — perhaps he can pledge $35 a month.

As mailing lists get larger, less and less attention is paid to finding duplicates or making sure the address is current. Donors may receive three or four copies of a mailing — one to Kate Hernandez, another to Francis Moreno and Kate Hernandez, a third to K. Hernandez and a fourth to Francis and Kate Moreno. Each of these names will reflect a gift that Kate made and how she signed her response card, or which checking account she wrote the check on. While some donors will call your attention to this, many more will mean to but will not take the time, and others who don't understand the limits of "merge and purge" technology will cease to give altogether.

Sometimes the lack of attention presents an even greater missed opportunity for the organization. The following story has happened in one version or another several times to organizations I have consulted with. A donor sends in a gift of $50. The check is separated from the return card and given to the finance person. The information on the card is entered into the database. "Joe Burgo, $100, 9/9, in response to spring appeal." However, the check said, "Howard Family Foundation." A quick search at the Foundation Center would show that the Howard Family Foundation gives away $2 million a year and that Joe H. Burgo is on the board, along with a number of other Burgos and Howards. Most organizations don't find any of this out because they don't search the checks for information other than the amount given. Sometimes this can be embarrassing. Suppose you haven't made the connection between Joe Burgo and the Howard Family Foundation and your foundation research independently shows the Howard Family Foundation to be a good prospect.

You write a proposal and are asked to make a presentation. Joe is at the presentation and seems surprised that you don't know that he is already a donor to your group.

Finally, as a group gets bigger, even larger donors begin to be neglected.

I gave $200 a year to a group for about four years. The first year, someone visited me and asked for the gift. The second year, someone called and asked me to renew. The third year, I got a personalized form letter. That year I didn't give for several months because I misplaced the letter. So, the fourth year, my personalized form letter came only three months after I had given my third-year's gift. I sent in $100 with a note that I would send the other $100 in a few months. I was never reminded of that pledge and forgot about it until the fifth year, when I got a form letter (not personalized) asking me to renew my gift in the range of $25–$100. Obviously, for that organization, people giving $100 or less are in a different system than those giving more than $100. I elected to be in the group that gives nothing and have never been asked again.

THE GREAT BALANCING ACT

How can we balance all the work that needs to be done — which is, after all, what donors are paying us to do — with cultivating the positive response most humans have to gestures of appreciation and noticing further fundraising opportunities in the clues our donors give us?

There are several solutions, which all begin with the fact that gratitude and appreciation have got to be values in the organizational culture. I can hear shouts of outrage: "I'm not going to kiss up to them!" "They should be grateful that we do the work we do!" "For crying out loud, I am not crawling on hands and knees to these people." I can see the gestures — loud slurping sounds, hands raised in begging postures, tongues hanging out like happy dogs.

Let me explain what I mean. It is true that the people who give us money year after year are grateful that we do the work we do. That's why they support us. But, as organizations, we need to understand our gratitude to them — they chose our group when they had thousands of other choices; they chose to give away some of their money when they could have used it in other ways; and they chose to do it year after year. I appreciate that. I value generosity in myself and in others. And, like most people, I value a bit of personal attention. In most cities, a person can go to the bank, the gas station, and even the grocery store without interacting with another person. Simply stick in your card and push the right buttons. With catalog shopping and the Internet, people can buy almost anything without leaving home. While this may be making life more convenient, it is also making people much more isolated.

People like to be noticed for their positive actions and are more likely to repeat such actions if they feel they make a difference. Personal attention in the form of notes, phone calls or even visits are the only way donors have of knowing that we have noticed their individual gift. Of course they know that as a group they make a difference. But, sometimes each donor wants to know, "Does my gift help? Did my individual gift mean anything to you?"

Once you are clear that your relationship to all your donors reflects some of your values as a person and the values of the organization, then your goal is to look for logistically feasible ways to be in touch because that is what you want to do, not what you feel you must do in order to get the money.

HOW TO TAKE CARE OF YOURSELF AND YOUR DONORS

Here are a number of ways you can insure against taking donors for granted and improve your own functioning:

1. *Make sure your database program is adequate.* You should not be hampered in your ability to keep track of donor information, including patterns of giving, because your database is too limited, too old, can't sort quickly, can't hold much information or whatever. You don't need to spend thousands of dollars on a database program, but you do need to take the time to find one that works for your group and then take the time to learn all that it can do. Many times a database can do a lot more than we are aware of but we have only learned enough to fulfill our basic needs. (See the sidebar on page 31.)

2. *Write, or have volunteers write, personal thank-you notes.* The body of the thank you can be the same, but at the bottom there should be a note from someone just saying, "Thanks again," or "Hope to meet you one of these days." With a good database program, you can enter the donor's gift and push a couple of buttons to generate a printed thank-you note. Then add a handwritten personal note to that one.

3. *Whoever does the data entry needs to be trained* to look for the following things, and then to code them in some way or bring them to someone's attention:

   a) Frequent giving. If a donor gives every time they are asked, or several times a year, they need to be thanked for that, as well as for each gift. You should consider visiting them or asking them to become part of a pledge program.

   b) An unusually large gift after a series of smaller ones. If a donor suddenly gives $200 or $500 when they have been giving $35 or $50, call them to thank them. Show that you notice. Pay attention to what they tell you about the gift.

You may want to visit this person for an even bigger gift. Also, when someone increases their gift dramatically, find out what the organization has done that they liked so much.

c) Notes that come with a check. People who take the time to tell you something, even if it is a Post-it with "Keep up the good work!" need to be noted. Your thank you can refer to their note. Also, accommodate their requests. If they say, "Only ask me once a year," or "Please don't phone me," then do what they wish.

d) Any interesting information on the check. In our example, Joe Burgo's check was drawn off of a trust. It may be drawn off of a small business or a corporation. In that case, note the name of the business and the need to research whether there is more money there. People sometimes tell you their professions on their checks: "Mary Jones, Esq.," or "Vin Hang, M.D.," or "Phyllis Browne, LCSW." Sometimes their checks will show something that the person believes in: "Pro-choice" or "Save the cougars." Again, these things may indicate interests, beliefs or ability to make a bigger gift. The check may tell you something about the household of the donor, such as the spouse or partner's name.

All of this information should be entered into the database, but it also has to be used. Data entry must be seen as a key fundraising function. If you have a person who does data entry, teach them about prospect research and emphasize the need to make your organization a welcoming environment for donors. If you do the data entry yourself, don't do it when you are tired or rushed.

4. Don't promise anything on the front end that you cannot fulfill on the back end. Many times organizations raise donors' expectations by how they cultivate and solicit the gift, but do not follow through with the same level of attention after the gift is received. This is probably nowhere more obvious than with foundations. Someone from the organization will write an excellent letter of inquiry, visit the foundation staff, send a thank-you letter with more materials as needed, write a good proposal, call to see if anything else is needed and generally be attentive and polite. As soon as the grant comes through, they send nothing to the foundation besides the six-month report until the next year, when their attention starts again with an eye to additional funding.

A similar sequence may be played out with donors. Your attentiveness in order to get the funding makes the donor think you will be attentive otherwise. If you promise that you will keep in touch, do so. Make a note in your calendar to send a newspaper clipping or something relevant to your work every few months. Put the person on your mailing list and send them invitations to your Open House or other special events. What makes you appear obsequious, groveling and fake is when you do whatever it takes to get the money and nothing to appreciate having gotten it.

5. Spread the work out over more people. If you are a paid staff person in charge of fundraising, every time you are doing a task that an intelligent, reasonable person could also do with a little training, find that person and give them that training. Thank-you notes, foundation research, phone calls to invite people to events or thank them for donations and so on can be done by volunteers, interns and board members. While it won't save you a lot of time because you will have to train and then supervise those workers, your helper may notice things that you don't, and you have involved more people in the work of the organization.

6. Keep your list clean. Once a year, print out your whole mailing list (if it is huge, you may have to do it in sections). With the help of people who have been around the organization for a long time, go through the list name by name. Look for typos, duplicate entries, people who are now deceased or divorced. The data entry person should be instructed to look for this type of information as well.

7. Make sure you and the organization understand that the purpose of fundraising is building relationships, not raising money. Obviously, money raised has to be one of the ways the fundraising program is evaluated, but it also must be evaluated in terms of number of new donors, retention rate (which is a good indicator of donor loyalty), number of new and renewing major donors, number of people involved in fundraising and general attitude toward fundraising on the part of everyone in the organization. Donors get neglected and relationships are sacrificed when fundraisers are under inordinate and inappropriate pressure to produce cash rather than to build a community of donors.

Using Strategies Effectively Over Time

INTRODUCTION

When I turned 35, I started not feeling as healthy as I wanted to. I decided to begin exercising regularly. I have made this decision regularly every since. I can report than my decision making muscles are in excellent shape from the many repetitions I put them through. However, because of my travel schedule, workload and a proclivity for reading or sleeping over running or swimming, I have never actually exercised regularly for more than a few weeks at a time. People who exercise a lot tell me that if you exercise long enough, you will get to a point that your body will prefer to exercise than not to. I think I have always quit exercising the day before that was going to happen.

Because of my adventures in exercise, I have a great deal of sympathy for organizations that have the same experience with fundraising. Like my friends who exercise regularly, I know that if you persist in your fundraising efforts, the same number of people working the same amount of time will raise more money every year. But getting to that point requires understanding how strategies work, what you need to consider as your organization gets older, how to vary your fundraising routine, when to drop a strategy and when to start something brand new.

The final section of this book explores philosophical and practical issues of raising money over the long haul.

nine

Fundraising and Strategic Planning

By the time your organization is five years old, your staff and board should know at least the rudiments of how to create a fundraising plan that will cover the next year or two. If nothing else, you do what you did the previous year, incorporating whatever you learned by doing it. In this way, you can usually raise as much money in the next year or two as you did the previous year, and probably more. If you have been paying attention to your attrition rate, if you have a decent acquisition program in place and if at least a few of your board or staff members are visiting at least a few of your major donors every year, then predicting small changes from year to year should not be too difficult.

While this "historical" method of planning may work in the short term, it will only take you so far. There are two problems with it: it doesn't allow for much growth or creativity, and it assumes that things are going to stay pretty much the same. They should not. When you project steady growth year after year, if you are successful all you wind up with is a bigger group. If you are not successful, all you wind up with is a smaller group.

Organizations need to ask more pressing questions than, "How big should our budget be next year?" or the even more deadly, "How much money can we raise next year?" They need to frame all questions in the context of their mission and goals. The basic question, "What is the most mission-fulfilling work we can take on?" produces a series of other questions, such as, what has changed since we started our organization — in our community, the economy, the world, the visibility of our issues today as compared to when we started, or even as compared to last year? What do we want to accomplish in the next five to 10 years? Only after the pressing questions have been raised and answered would you ask budget questions, beginning with this question: "Where do we want to get our money? Who do we want to belong to?" After that is settled you will ask, "How much will it cost to be the group we want to be?" The answer to all these questions are the basis for an organization's strategic — or long-range — plan. That is a plan that will incorporate the best actions to get you to your goals over the next several years. From that, you can develop a strategic fundraising plan.

A strategic plan is a flexible document, more likely to contain guidelines than rules. Once begun, the strategic planning process is a continuous one, so that at the end of each year progress is evaluated and the plan is modified and extended by another year. Unless there is a dramatic shift in the nature of the organization's work, there should never be a need to start a strategic planning process over again. Some planning consultants make a distinction between strategic planning and long-range planning. I will let them duke this out in their own books and monographs. As used here, a strategic plan can cover as short a time as six months or as long a time as five years or more. Short or long, the strategic plan gives critical guidance to the development function and should make development easier.

If one were to conduct a random survey of development people and ask for their true response to the words "strategic planning" or "long-range planning" as applied to fundraising, one would most likely hear some or all of the following responses: "Necessary," "Should do it," "Tedious," "Never works," "Tried that," "Board wants it," "Funder wants it." Few people would say, "Exciting!" "So helpful!" "Couldn't live without it!" "Love those plans!" We have mixed feelings about planning because although we can see in theory that creating a plan should help our work, too often our experience is that it rarely does and that the further out an organization plans, the less resemblance the plans have to reality. As a friend said, "There's the plan and then there is what happened."

Nevertheless, there are ways to make planning for fundraising helpful and reality-based, so that the plans actually do shape the future.

The first step, as I have indicated, is to create an organizational strategic plan. A strategic plan begins with the case statement, and the case statement begins with the mission. After five years of analyzing more than 1,000 nonprofits for what contributes to excellence, the Independent Sector concluded that having a clear sense of mission was primary. Along with the mission there had to be a strategic plan.

There are many good resources on how to create a strategic plan (see bibliography). Suffice it to say here that without a strategic plan the fundraising plan becomes the driving vision of the organization, which means that over time an organization is driven by where it can get money rather than by what it should be doing. There are a number of these groups in the nonprofit community — taking up space, soaking up resources, producing little that is significant. They have grown old without maturing, and have confused existing with accomplishing.

MAKING SURE YOU'RE IN THE RIGHT PLACE

Once a strategic organizational plan is in place, fundraising planning can begin. Fundraising planning also starts with philosophical, mission-based considerations. I was once asked to help a group create a long-range fundraising plan. They had received money from a foundation to create this plan and the foundation promised that once the group had the plan, the foundation would provide seed money to start implementing it. The condition the foundation imposed and the group agreed to was that the plan had to move the group from relying on foundations for 90% of its income to relying on a broad base of individual donors for that 90%, and this move had to be completed in three years. With a budget of $250,000, the group was being challenged to go from raising $25,000 from individuals to raising $225,000 from individuals (or more, if their budget grew).

I met with the executive director, the development director and a small committee of the board. We convened in a large conference room and when I arrived, sheets of white paper were taped around the room, each person had a pencil and a calculator and they were ready to go. I began the meeting by posing the following two scenarios and asking them to write down their responses privately:

1. Suppose there is a person among your donors who is at the tail end of a terminal illness and has made your group the beneficiary of her sizable estate. Once her estate is settled, your group will receive enough money to yield $200,000 in interest every year. Would you still want to undertake this individual donor program?

2. Suppose we can predict accurately that your group will be successful in the fundraising effort we are here to plan, but that you would also be successful raising money from foundations, and that your luck with foundations would never run out. Would you still want to undertake this individual donor program?

After a few minutes, I asked the group to share their thoughts. In response to the first scenario, most agreed that they would embark on this donor program anyway, but would give themselves more than three years to make the change. They felt the endowment money could be used for major expansion, such as buying a building, upgrading salaries or expanding programs.

The responses to the second scenario were more provocative and revealed a division in the group. The development director said he would not undertake this plan at all. He pointed out that his job was going to change dramatically as he was being asked to go from something he was good at (researching foundations, writing proposals and maintaining relationships with funders) to something he knew little about. The executive director also said she wished the second scenario were true, but she didn't see the point of taking time to discuss it. "The handwriting is on the wall," she said. "We have no choice but to move to this individual donor thing."

The board members were more enthusiastic. One felt that there was too much pressure on the staff to produce money and that the organization depended too heavily on the development director. Another felt that the organization would be much freer to say and do what it wanted if it were less reliant on foundation funding, including being able to choose issues because they were important rather than primarily because they were fundable. A third board member had a mixed reaction. "It means a lot more work for the board members," she said, "and if we don't do our work, it will result in even more work for the staff."

The executive director pressed me again, "Why are we having this conversation? We have made an agreement with this foundation to do this work, and we came here to spell out the tasks."

I said, "We are discussing these issues because if, in your organizational heart, you would prefer to be supported by a few foundations, then all the planning in the world is not going to help you move in another direction. You have to believe that building a broad base of individual support is exactly what should be done, even if you had other options."

Many groups embark on a plan to diversify their funding base because it sounds good in theory, or because their funders told them to, or because they thought they had no choice. But as with any big life choice — going to college, buying a house, taking a new job — if the person making the choice doesn't really want to do it, then they are probably not going to do it very well (see Lesson Six in Section One: "The Importance of Process"). In the case of an organization moving to individual donor support, without wholehearted commitment, the donors will be neglected, the development office will experience constant turnover, the executive director will be resentful and overworked, and not enough money will be raised.

THE PLANNING PROCESS

If, as discussed in Chapter One, your group has decided to seek most of its income from a broad base of donors, then you are ready to create a fundraising plan that can be incorporated into the strategic plan.

The strategic plan should give the fundraising planning team a fairly clear sense of the amount of money that will be required over the next three to five years to accomplish the work that has been laid out and in what increments the program is expected to grow. Is a steady increase planned every year, or will next year require a capital campaign to acquire a facility in order to conduct the programs planned for the following years? What kind of staffing will be needed? What about equipment? Because the array of technology required to run a nonprofit is always increasing, a healthy amount should be budgeted for computers, software, and things not yet invented.

The first step is to do an assessment of what you have in place now so you can determine what you will need to put into place before you can undertake to expand your fundraising goals. It will then be a fairly simple matter of filling in the tasks required to get there.

Fundraising Assessment

In addition to looking at the criteria laid out in Chapter One on healthy fundraising programs, consider the following questions:

a) Do you have a full-time person (paid or volunteer) whose job is coordinating the fundraising efforts of your organization? If your organization's budget is more than $500,000, do you have support staff or volunteer assistance equal to at least another half-time person devoted to development?

b) Does your budget include money for training related to development?

c) Does your budget include money for a consultant to help you with development strategies such as planned giving and capital campaigns, or with converting a database or finding lists for direct mail?

d) Is your technology up-to-date, and are the people using the technology up-to-date on how to use it?

e) Do you have a current brochure? Annual Report? Wish list?

f) Do you have a newsletter? Does it come out on time? Is it valuable and useful?

g) Do you have an up-to-date historical collection of special event invitations, direct mail appeals, foundation proposals, press clippings?

h) Do you have a current list of board members, staff members and key volunteers, including name, address and brief biography?

Next, reflect on the overall state of fundraising in your organization. I have found few organizations where fundraising went smoothly, but it is helpful if you are not always leaping from crisis to crisis. While development people usually feel that their work is never done, they need to be able to limit their work to a 40- to 50-hour week. Perennial overtime simply disguises the cost of doing business. If it always takes you 60 hours a week to do your job, then your job is actually a job and a half. If you quit and someone is hired who does not wish to work 150% for full-time pay, they will appear to be less efficient than you were. Plus, constantly working overtime will make you tired and frustrated and you will get less done as you get more burned out.

Any substantial plans for increasing the number and range of individual donors need to be postponed until the problems with your current development set-up are either solved or you have a solution in sight. If, for example, you find it impossible to get your newsletter out on time and you acquire more donors, then you simply have more people wondering why they never hear from you — or, more likely, forgetting about you altogether and joining another group. There is no point in seeking publicity that generates calls from people wanting more information if your brochure is out of date and out of print. There is no point in expanding your donor list if your database is ill equipped to handle the number of donors you have now.

Strategy Planning Grid

After you have done an assessment and planned how you will shore up your infrastructure, you are ready to project fundraising strategies out a few years. The first step is to create a grid based on the three functions of fundraising: acquiring donors, retaining them and getting some of them to give more. For each category, you then plan what to do. Note what you are doing that works and what you might like to move into. It's good to experiment with new strategies from time to time. For this step, don't think in terms of time-frame or you will censor yourself about what you might like to try. Here's an example:

STRATEGIES EMPLOYED & OUTCOMES

Function	Always worked	Usually worked	Consider Adding
Acquisition	Trading names	Asking donors for names	Web page
	Street fair sign-up	Raffle	House parties
Retention	Renewal letters	Phone lapsed donors	Set up EFT
	Extra appeals	Phone for special project	Canvass
	Envelope in newsletter	—	E-mail newsletter
	Auction	Dinner/Dance	Small soirees
Upgrade			
Donors of $500+	Personal solicitation	—	Gift club
Donors of $100 – $500	Personal solicitation	—	—
All donors	—	—	Twice-a-year planned giving mailing

After you create your grid, create a full set of tasks and a timeline for each item on the grid that you have decided to do, plus a budget showing the front money required to start this strategy. When completed, your fundraising plan, with timelines, task lists and budgets, will probably cover several pages or spreadsheets.

Fundraising success will be measured by the following results:

1. Amount of money raised
2. Number of new donors acquired
3. Number of donors retained
4. Number of donors upgraded
5. Number of volunteers and staff involved
6. Cost of each strategy compared to benefits

The last item needs some discussion. For common and widely used strategies, we can estimate costs using the following formula:

- Acquisition mailings: $1.00–$1.50 per $1.00 raised
- Renewal mailings: $.10–$.15 per $1.00 raised
- Extra appeals: $.20–$.25 per $1.00 raised
- Special events: cost varies widely but budget as high as $.50 per $1.00 raised
- Personal asking: cost varies widely but allow $.10 per $1.00 raised

If planned giving is one of your strategies, it will take five to seven years to see financial results, so for the first years you will have money going out but not coming in. Later, if you are successful, this will become one of the most inexpensive strategies because the gifts received are usually relatively large.

For the experimental strategies, such as Internet fundraising, you may have a large outlay in the beginning as you design your Web page, and it may take a year or two to figure out how to drive traffic to your site, establish links, and work out the glitches. Much of your success with the Web will depend on having someone who is always updating your site and keeping up with the technology.

Because so much is changing in fundraising, organizations must be willing to spend some money very experimentally and be willing to wait a few years to see results or to decide to abandon a strategy. Even as you look at the "always worked" column, think about whether something else would work better.

If you conceptualize your plan like a Web page, picture each strategy as an icon, which, if clicked on leads to more information — tasks, timeline, budget, costs, fundraising goals.

The final step is to put all your information on a calendar. Your fundraising plan should be projected over three to five years. The calendar for the first year will be the most detailed, with tasks for each month spelled out. The second year's plan will contain less detail, and so on through the fifth year. The key to this kind of planning is to *always* be able to look 12 months ahead. This means that every month or two, you evaluate the two months that have passed and add two months of detail onto your calendar. Whether you do this with spreadsheets or calendar software or sheets of paper with yellow Post-its, the point is to always be looking at the next 12 months.

All of this planning will be a worthless exercise if you do not build in a constant evaluation process. Every month that goes by, every quarter and every year, you need to see how well your plans corresponded with reality. What changes need to be made in your projections? Where are you ahead? Behind? What information do you need to get in order to know if a strategy is worth pursuing further?

The first few months of planning as intensively as I am recommending can be frustrating. Most of us tend to take on too much and underestimate how much time something will take and how many details can go wrong. Possibly we underbudgeted the costs or overestimated the profits. If you project high on your expenses and conservatively on your income, you will be saved from making financially disastrous mistakes. If you see your mistakes as information, then you can use them to avoid making them again. If you use your mistakes as a way to put yourself down ("I'm no good at planning") or to put others down ("My plan would work if I didn't have such a loser for an executive director"), then your planning process will just become another way to feel martyred and burned out.

If you make plans, keep track of what actually happened, create new plans based on your new knowledge, keep track of what you learned and so on, you will soon notice that planning is actually helpful, that plans and reality are related, and that planning can be fun.

ten

Savings Accounts, Reserve Funds and Endowments

As they age, most organizations, like most individuals, seek some level of financial stability. There are several ways to ensure some measure of financial security without falling into the traps of security at any cost described in Chapter Five. Too often, groups leap from spending whatever they raise to wanting to establish an endowment. This chapter explores some alternatives to endowments and also discusses what a group needs to have in place before setting up an endowment.

THREE PATHS TO SECURITY

There are three ways most smaller nonprofits can ensure an appropriate measure of financial stability: maintaining a savings account with few or no restrictions on its use; maintaining a reserve fund (or funds) with a defined use; and establishing a formal endowment with very clear guidelines for managing the principal and using the interest.

The differences among these measures are important and the way you finance each of them will vary. Some organizations use all three vehicles for saving money, some use only one, and some groups do not have any money set aside at all. Let's look at each strategy.

Savings Account: After your organization is a few years old and the donors who helped get you started have moved on to start something else and the foundations that granted you money have passed their honeymoon period and are increasingly less likely to give you new grants, you start experiencing financial ups and downs that are not related to being new. You realize that no matter how carefully you budget your expenses, there are unexpected costs. No matter how cautiously you put together your fundraising projections, you sometimes fall short.

At the same time, you begin to experience some predictability. Some donors give year after year. You can expect a certain level of response from your mail appeals. Some board members always call their prospects. With enough asking going on, you can count on a certain amount of money coming in. At this point, if they haven't done so already, smart groups open a savings account. They can literally open an account and move money into it steadily, or they can simply create a line item on their books indicating money that is in "savings." The money thus set aside can be used for any unexpected expense, shortfalls in the general operating budget or cash flow problems. Generally, it is not used to fund specific programs.

Reserve Funds: Money put in a reserve fund is usually designated for expenses that can be anticipated but their timing cannot be predicted. Community groups use reserve funds to put money aside for big campaigns, to fight SLAPP (Strategic Lawsuit Against Public Participation) suits if they can't get insurance to cover those costs, to generate media attention, to respond strongly to something that has happened in their community (an oil spill, an incidence of police brutality, exposure of a corrupt government official) or to front the money for an important event.

Endowment: Money in an endowment is set aside for an organization's permanent use. The principal of the endowment is invested and only a percentage of the money earned as interest is designated to be spent. Legally, the principal of an endowment can be spent under extraordinary circumstances, but this is to be avoided.

Let's look at one group that has all three of these savings vehicles in place.

Community Concern

Community Concern, a health advocacy group focussed primarily on AIDS education and prevention in the poorest neighborhoods of their city, rents a storefront office for $1 a month on a street where most businesses have had to close. The rent is kept at this token amount on the condition that the landlord doesn't have to do any internal repairs. He will replace things that wear out, but he will not pay to have anything fixed. Repairing the water heater or electrical wiring, painting, dealing with insulation and the like are up to the group.

The storefront is perfect for this group. It is wheelchair accessible, near a bus line and gives them visibility in the neighborhood they serve. The group has taken the money they were paying in rent on their previous space and put it into a savings account. They don't know what will go wrong with the building or when, but they know that eventually they will need to make some repairs. They also use the money in their savings to improve their offices. They have painted, bought a new refrigerator for the staff kitchen and purchased decent chairs for the meeting room.

The director can use the savings account for any expense up to $1,000, beyond that, a vote of the staff is required. Expenses must be reported to the board and cannot exceed the amount in the savings account.

Community Concern also has a reserve fund. They use the reserve fund to rent billboards during AIDS Awareness Week, to pay tuition for members to go to trainings, to hire a media firm to publicize their issues and to cover other expenses incurred during organizing campaigns. The reserve fund is called the "Oh My God! Fund," named after what the mayor said the first time the group bused 200 people to City Hall to protest the closing of a free health clinic in the neighborhood. They raise the money for the reserve fund from their membership in a yearly appeal describing what they have used the money for in the past, and asking people to make an extra gift to maintain the "Oh My God! Fund." It is one of their most popular appeals.

Like the savings account, the Oh My God! Reserve Fund can be used by staff for any expense of less than $1,000: Greater expenses must be approved by the board or its executive committee, whichever is meeting first. Since the board members are often involved in the decisions leading up to spending money from the reserve, a board member usually presents the idea to the rest of the board. The reserve fund money cannot be used for anything that the savings account would normally cover, but the savings account can augment costs incurred under the auspices of the reserve fund.

Two years ago a long-time donor to Community Concern died, having named the organization as a beneficiary of his life insurance. They received $10,000. They were touched both by their donor's generosity and by the size of the bequest. They decided to use the money to begin an endowment. They have decided not to draw any interest from the endowment until it has reached $100,000, and then to use 50% of the earnings for general operating expenses and reinvest the remaining 50%. Only the board can decide to invade the principal and then only if the entire board agrees that there is no other recourse and the organization is in danger of closing.

They advertise their endowment fund in their newsletter, asking donors to include Community Concern in their wills. They have approached a few donors for one-time large gifts for the endowment and have received one gift of $20,000 and two of $5,000. They spend little time on raising money for the endowment, seeing it as a long-term process that will largely be funded by bequests.

Community Concern would probably not have started an endowment at the time they did without the initial bequest. Their savings and reserve fund give them a measure of financial security. But they realized that one-time-only gifts like this bequest ought to be kept in an account that wouldn't be easily spent.

Community Concern is unusually thoughtful in its financial planning, but almost any group could follow their example, particularly in regard to their reserve fund.

HOW TO THINK ABOUT FINANCIAL STABILITY

Nonprofits face two problems when looking at ways to be more financially stable. The first arises from the standard of care that board members are expected to exercise in making financial decisions. Nonprofit law says that board members are to be "prudent" and tells them they have "fiduciary responsibility." The concept of prudence and fiduciary responsibility are often explained by saying that board members are to treat the nonprofit's money with the same care they would use in dealing with their own money. Some books call this care "stewardship."

However, many very good people are not that careful with their own money, and the standard of care they exercise is not one we wish to impose on a nonprofit. Few people are taught about responsible money management, and most live in a commercial culture that constantly urges us to buy on credit. As a result, most people carry credit card debt and few have any savings outside of their retirement plans, if they even have these.

The second problem for nonprofits is that financial security is always measured in terms of money: how much we have, how much interest we will earn, how much we have been promised by this foundation or that donor. We need to see other elements of our organization as assets that earn predictable amounts of money. For example, a 10-year-old organization with 1,000 donors monitors their attrition rate carefully. Every year they know exactly how many new donors they will need in order to replace those who have lapsed. Every year for the past five years they have netted at least $25,000 from donors giving less than $100, and $50,000 from their major donor campaign aimed at donors giving $100 or more. Last year, their best fundraising year ever, they netted $38,000 in gifts of less than $100, and $100,000 in gifts of $100 or more.

This organization, like many that I work with, wants to start an endowment in order to have some "predictable income." I point out that they already have predictable income — every year, if they invest a certain amount of time and money in their donors, they will net at least $100,000 and probably more. To be able to take $100,000 a year from an endowment would require principal of about $2 million.

Donors are a source of financial stability. If your group knows it can raise a certain amount of money from its donors, questions before you are how much more money do you need, and will it be easier to get that money from an investment than from having more donors?

Once you understand that income from donors is predictable, your fundraising plans become built around getting more donors and offering them more and more ways to help you. These ways may include asking them for capital gifts, for bequests, or for other planned gifts. Some of the donors will want to contribute to a reserve fund or an endowment if they think your group will be strengthened by having such vehicles.

Groups that have not previously had much experience with setting money aside should start with something simple, like a savings account. The discussion of what it is to be used for, who can decide when it can be spent and how much can be taken out at any given time, as well as how the savings account is to be financed and invested, will give you practice for the much larger discussion you will have to have if you decide to begin an endowment. You may find that a savings account gives you enough stability to eliminate the need for more complicated strategies.

WHAT TO CONSIDER IN STARTING AN ENDOWMENT

Many organizations that have taken the first steps of having a savings account and a reserve fund may now want to consider an endowment. Here are the good things about an endowment besides just having the money:

1. **Planning.** An endowment allows, actually even forces, an organization to think in terms of long-range planning because an endowment means you have committed the group to exist in perpetuity.

2. **Larger gifts.** Endowments provide a vehicle for people to make larger gifts to an organization than might be appropriate for an annual gift, and they allow people to make one-time-only gifts with assurance that the gift won't just be spent.

3. **Bequest gifts.** An endowment is a vehicle for people to express their commitment to an organization through their wills; few people will leave money to an organization that does not have some kind of permanent fund.

4. **Improved credit.** Endowment principal can be used for capital expenses and as collateral for loans, if ever needed. Some groups have used some of their endowment principal to buy a building for their offices.

For every good thing you can say about endowments, you can find some problems. Here are the most common drawbacks to having an endowment:

1. **Unearned longevity.** Because they allow an organization to exist permanently, endowments may support organizations that ought to have gone out of business.

2. *Reduced accountability.* When endowments are very large, they allow organizations to become unresponsive to the community. With a large guaranteed annual income, groups may cease to try to involve their community and may be impervious to criticism. Grassroots organizations often eschew endowments for that reason.

3. **Misguided complacency.** Endowments can provide a false sense of security, since interest rates can vary, stock markets can fall, and money can be invested badly.

4. **Deflected donations.** The existence of an endowment may discourage some donors from giving annual gifts if they perceive that other organizations need the money more.

5. **Outdated direction.** When donors endow certain programs, the work of the organization can become donor-driven rather than mission-driven. This is, of course, a problem with foundation and government funding or any large single source of designated funding. However, the complication with an endowment is that the donor is usually dead by the time it is clear that the program is no longer needed. Changing the terms of how the money can be spent is often complicated, legally messy and expensive.

Most of the problems involved with an endowment can be avoided if an organization thoroughly debates and unanimously answers two questions: First, does everyone in the organization agree that the group should exist permanently? And second, what will endowment income be used for?

Most organizations are formed with the idea that their work will be so successful that they will put themselves out of business. When domestic violence programs, food banks and homeless shelters seek to be endowed, they give the message that they have ceased trying to eradicate these problems and that battered, abused, hungry and homeless people are a permanent feature of our society. Groups working for a just society must maintain the idea that they will be able to address the root cause of social problems and eventually eliminate the problem they are focussed on.

Some organizations are designed to be permanent features of the nonprofit landscape — arts and culture groups, alternative schools, independent publications, community centers, historic preservation societies, land trusts, parks, libraries and the like are designed to exist forever. The degree to which they should be supported by tax dollars rather than private charitable contributions might be debated, but an endowment would be appropriate for any group doing work that will always be needed or wanted.

There are many groups that can envision a society in which their work would not be needed and are working for the creation of that society, but they must admit that this society will probably not exist for at least 50 years. That means that people not yet born will someday be sitting on the board or working on the staff of these groups. The current board feels an obligation to its future leadership to make life a little easier financially and a permanent source of funding to augment fundraising efforts would certainly do that.

If your group decides that permanence, or at least a few generations of existence are required, it now discusses use of the interest and the investment of the principal of the endowment. These questions don't have to be entirely sorted out, and when they are answered, it will have to be done with an element of flexibility, but those people who imagine that their fundraising burden will be less because of endowment income will have to come to an agreement with those people who see the endowment income as a vehicle for doing more programs and expanding beyond what they are currently able to raise. This discussion about what to do with the interest will inform the size of the endowment the group aims for and the methods it will use to raise endowment funds. Will you go the route of Community Concern and simply let the endowment grow? Will you conduct a full-scale endowment campaign? The how-tos of creating an endowment are explored in a number of books, including my book, *Fundraising for Social Change* (see bibliography).

The process of deciding on what financial stability would look like for your group, what strategy to use in pursuing it, how to make sure your financial planning is mission-driven, how to think for the long term, and how long is long term are all important questions to discuss. It may take months to achieve consensus, but it is worth the time. These kinds of discussions strengthen the only real lasting endowment your group has — the passion and commitment of the activists, whether staff or volunteers, and the creation of similar passion in new people.

eleven

NONPROFIT DOES NOT EQUAL ANTI-PROFIT:

Getting Comfortable with Making Money

I think I can say without exaggeration that I have heard every conceivable myth about what nonprofits are and are not legally allowed to do with money. These have been told to me by board members, staff members — even consultants. I have been told that nonprofits cannot legally earn any money, pay salaries, invest money, earn interest, or borrow money. That they must always sell things for less than what they cost, cannot have credit cards or own buildings. I have been told that people who work for nonprofits must be bonded and that they are always allowed to fly for half-price. One woman told me seriously that people who work for nonprofits shouldn't give blood because they don't eat right and tend to be anemic. When I asked her why they don't eat right she said, "Because they can't afford decent food."

While most of the groups I have worked with closely have known that none of these so-called rules are true, many have felt uncomfortable with the idea of charging an appropriate amount for a product, an event, a consultation, a training or a service. Some have epitomized the business school joke, "We sold each product at a loss, but we made it up in volume."

Many have written about the profound psychological and sociological reasons that people who work for nonprofits feel uncomfortable making a profit. These reasons spring from a culture that treats money as a taboo and from a warped belief that to be in service to others is to eschew money altogether. Those of us who believe that class, like race and gender, is a key factor in understanding our world and must be addressed in working for structural change and social justice bring another kind of ambivalence about making money to the picture. We act as though charging money to attend a conference is extortion, or that making a profit on a special event puts us in bed with multinational arms merchants. Too easily, we lose sight of the scale we are working on and the motives we are working from.

Raising money effectively requires becoming comfortable with money — asking for money, thanking people for money given, and making money — in fact making enough of a profit on our mail appeals, events, solicitations, products, grant proposals and so on that we have enough money to do the rest of our work.

The following two stories show groups coming to an appropriate understanding of the role of profit in their overall fundraising planning.

CASE STUDIES

Product Glut

Two years ago, I was invited to consult with a children's advocacy group in Chicago. I met them in their tiny, crowded office, where three staff members shared one room. They showed me around, which took 10 seconds. They had a second room of equal size to their office that they used for storage. They also had two large storage closets. Since these spaces were jam-packed with boxes, I asked what they were storing. Sheepishly, they showed me. One closet had 500 mugs bearing their logo, nicely boxed and neatly stacked. The other closet had hundreds of T-shirts in many sizes and colors, printed with a slight variation of the logo that appeared on the mugs. The second room held a few thousand copies of a book they had published.

Their one-room office had to hold everything they needed to run their programs, including all their office supplies and reference books as well as the usual filing cabinets, desks and computers, because all their storage spaces were full of products theoretically for sale. I say theoretically because, although the group was willing to sell their products, they didn't advertise them anywhere other than in their newsletter. "But," as one staff member told me, "this stuff is not our problem because it is already paid for. Our problem is how to raise more money."

Bargains Galore

Later that year, I was invited to do some board and staff training during an annual meeting of the Long Run Planning Coalition, an environmental justice organization in a small city in Colorado. The meeting ran over a weekend, and on Saturday evening, the group held their annual auction. Offering to help set up, I went with a staff person and two board members to the organization's office to get the auction items. We loaded up a van with an impressive assortment of framed wildlife photographs, homemade preserves in fancy jars, two new mountain bikes, a quilt, and a number of gift certificates for bed and breakfasts, guided canoe trips, horseback riding seminars and the like. That night, about 200 people came to the auction. As there were no minimum bids required, some items went for incredibly low prices.

I talked to several people at the auction who said they came every year. They loved the bargains. I asked a few people if they knew anything about the group sponsoring the auction. "Good group," one said, "they work with children, right?" Another said, "I think this is the group that saves wild horses." A third said, "They are a bunch of tree-huggers, but they know how to put on an auction."

The auction grossed $12,000 and netted $10,000, which pleased the group's board members immensely. The fact that the items that were auctioned off had a combined value of $25,000 pleased them even more — as one board member said, "People have a good time, get great bargains and we make money. Not much you can do to improve that."

These two stories have a lot in common. A group that thinks their storage rooms full of unsold goods have nothing to do with fundraising and a group that thinks it is good fundraising to let auction items go for less than half of their value both have the same problem — they have not thought about what they want from the strategy they are using, and they wind up with much less money than they deserve for the amount of work they are doing.

I have seen this syndrome hundreds of times. It has a variety of faces: a group will put on a conference, but not charge a large enough fee per participant to cover costs; a group will send speakers to other meetings for no fee regardless of the requesting group's ability to pay; tickets to an event will be priced well below the market rate "so that no one will feel excluded"; products will be created but with no marketing plan and a general discomfort about selling, the products will be stored until they are eventually given away or discarded.

Unlike many bad habits, the habit of raising less money than you can is a fairly easy one to change. The way to do it is as follows: before embarking on any strategy in which money will be given to your group in exchange for a product, a service, or an event, and not as a general donation, answer the following questions:

1. Who are we trying to reach?

2. What do we hope the people reached will do?

3. Are we willing to be criticized, and by whom?

4. Are we willing to say no, and to whom?

5. What are all the ways we can make money on this strategy?

6. What are our goals besides money, or is there another way to raise this money and meet our other goals besides this strategy?

7. How much money are we trying to raise?

Let's look at our two examples and see what the groups would do differently using these questions.

The Children's Advocacy Project has three products they have developed over the years. The mugs were created as a give-away for a conference where they had hoped to have 500 people. However, only 50 people signed up, and many of those asked for a scholarship, so the group decided to sell the mugs at the conference. Only five mugs sold.

The group's T-shirts were created to sell at street fairs and to give to donors as a premium for gifts of $50 or more. One donor gave $50 in order to get the T-shirt. When he saw that he could have bought the T-shirt at a fair for $16 and renewed his membership for $25, saving $9, he complained that the group was gouging its members. In the face of that one criticism, the group decided to discontinue selling the T-shirts. Another member complained that giving a premium for a larger gift was elitist; since she was on the board, the group decided to discontinue having T-shirts as a premium. Not being able to sell them or use them as a premium, but not being willing to give them away, the group ended up storing the T-shirts.

The book grew out of successful trainings on the rights of children that the group had developed for public interest lawyers. The training was popular and they were asked to teach social workers, teachers, and even a class of clergy. The foundation that had funded developing the training suggested the group write a book based on their curriculum and sell it. They did. They had 5,000 copies printed. They sold 200 copies to the previous training participants and now they give the book out as part of their trainings, which accounts for 100 books a year. They have 4,500 copies of the book left and are afraid that if the books don't sell in the next two years, the text will begin to go out-of-date. They don't know how to market the book and have thought of giving it away, but they don't know who they would give it to. With no process to figure out what to do, they are just storing the books.

By first asking, "Who are we trying to reach with our mug, T-shirt or book?" the group would see that a mug and T-shirt are created primarily to raise the visibility of the group. Their instinct to give them away or sell them as part of another event was correct, but they did not keep at it. Instead, they wilted in the face of two criticisms. But if you increase your visibility, which is a requirement of successful fundraising, you run a higher risk of being criticized.

There will always be someone who criticizes anything you do that has to do with money. It is important to listen to these criticisms in case they contain a legitimate point, but most of the time the criticism is based on an invalid premise. For example, a thank-you gift (newsletter, T-shirt, bumper sticker) for a membership or other donation is not intended to be equal to the value of the donation — in fact, the benefits given to a donor are to be of negligible value in the marketplace, or the group would have to deduct the value of the item from the value of the donation. A person who gives $50 and gets a T-shirt as a thank you is not meant to think that the value of the T-shirt plus the value of the newsletter or other membership benefits are equal to their $50.

The idea that it is elitist to give premiums for slightly larger donations comes from the mistaken belief that people who give more money have more money. In fact, people who give more money may or may not have more money, but they are demonstrating that they care more about the group. The difference between $20 for a regular membership and $50 for a membership that includes a free T-shirt is insignificant and trivializes the meaning of elitism. People who are willing to pay an extra $20–$25 are good candidates for helping to increase the visibility of a group because they are likely to wear a T-shirt or use a mug at their office, and to talk about the group to their friends. Elitism is when people have to make a minimum donation of $1,000 to be on a board of directors, or when the only donors listed as givers in an annual report are those who gave $250 or more. Elitism is when grantmakers are invited to informational breakfasts, but long-time volunteers are not, or when clients are not asked for money because the group assumes they don't have any money.

Often, simply explaining the rationale behind a fee or a premium will quell objections. The donor who raises the objection may just be having a bad day or may not have thought through the meaning of his comment. The group also needs to examine the language that it uses to promote premiums, so that donors are clear that they are being asked for a bigger donation and they will be thanked with a token gift. This will help avoid misunderstandings.

The other mistake the group made with these items was that no one knew how to market them. I worked with them on a plan that developed several marketing actions. First, they offered both the T-shirt and the mug as premiums to higher donors. They also advertised them for sale in their newsletter and included a little picture of them. Third, they joined with four other groups in their neighborhood and persuaded a store that sells coffee, coffee beans, espresso machines, mugs and so on to do a three-day display and sale called, "Support Good Work." The four groups displayed a number of items for sale, including hand towels, hats, reusable plastic picnic cups and, of course, mugs and T-shirts. The store took a small handling charge for dealing with the sales and the sales tax. The store loved the publicity and the groups made a profit as well as increasing their visibility. "Support Good Work" is now a yearly event.

The book that Children's Advocacy published is in a different category from the other two items. First of all, it has market value. It is a serious book and its primary purpose is not advertising the work of the group. The marketing plan for the book included sending a summary of it with a cover letter offering a free copy to instructors in social work schools, law schools and public health programs throughout the country who might consider using it in their courses. More than two dozen picked up the book as a course textbook. The group also decided to offer the book at 50% discount to other groups working for children's rights. Child abuse prevention programs, public interest law firms and domestic violence programs got a letter, a summary of the book, and a return form with a return envelope. The group mailed 5,000 letters and got 150 orders (an excellent 3% response), with a total of 400 books sold.

In addition to moving their book, the group now has a much bigger mailing list of people and organizations to whom they can advertise their seminars or approach for donations. Now that the book is selling, they need to decide whether to bring it up-to-date and republish it, offer it to a publisher or let it go out of print.

Finally, the group has spiffed up their Web page, so that it now includes the book, the T-shirt and the mugs for sale. As a result of all these actions, they have cleared out their storage room and can now use it for an office. But more important, they understand that even though the products were paid for, they were still costing money by taking up space and the organization was not recouping any of the money that had been spent. The group realized that investing in products that they would not sell was a poor use of money and was not good stewardship of the money they had been given. This group has agreed not to create any more products without setting goals for their distribution, and creating a serious marketing plan ahead of time.

The Long Run Planning Coalition is better at marketing than the Children's Advocacy Project, but they fall down in the area of setting prices at their popular auction. They exhibit the same reluctance in their membership program. Membership dues are $5 a year. They arrive at this price by dividing the production, printing and mailing costs of the newsletter (which is a benefit of membership) by the number printed and adding $2 for the cost of advertising the Annual General Meeting. Most of their members send $10 voluntarily and always remark how low the membership dues are. Their 300 members give about $3,000 in membership contributions every year.

The auction is the group's biggest fundraiser, and it does well. However, every year some of the donors of auction items complain that the items are being sold for far too little. Some donors have simply started sending money instead of giving an item, but others feel disrespected and have stopped giving Long Run anything at all.

Long Run is largely supported by foundation grants from foundations on the East Coast. The board of the coalition does not feel the need to bring in money from a broad base of donors. The $15,000–$20,000 they make every year from their member dues and events takes the edge off financially and keeps them in touch with people in their surrounding geographic community, but most of their serious fundraising effort is done by the executive director, who writes foundation proposals and reports and makes one or two trips a year to visit foundations in New York and Washington.

The board and staff of Long Run had asked me to conduct a training on how to ask for money, and so were surprised when I told them they didn't need that training. Obviously, they were perfectly able to ask for as much money as they wanted. However, I asked them three questions: First, why did they want so little from their members? Second, why were they not concerned about year after year gradually alienating the small business community and the artists who donated their auction items? And third, what did they think about primarily being known as an organization that was cheap to belong to and where you could get great bargains at events?

The board chair explained that the main reason they charge for membership at all was that a foundation suggested it, and the reason they had their auction was that it was fun and it was a way to let local people buy stuff that usually only tourists could afford. The executive director concurred, and added that if they raised a lot more money from their community she feared the foundations would give less. "Foundations have a lot more money than we do, and it is easy to get," she said. I had known that my way was being paid by a foundation grant, and now asked the question I should have asked before I came: "Why did you decide to do this training?" The reply was predictable: "Our program officer suggested it."

The rest of the afternoon was spent in a difficult but lively discussion about the fact that most of their fundraising effort was aimed at pleasing funders. That was their real audience, that was their market, that was who they hoped would produce their funding. The members, the donors, the buyers were all tools toward that end. Once it was spelled out so clearly, no one felt comfortable being so focused on foundation giving, but they did not necessarily want to give up being completely accessible to their community. We arrived at a plan that pleased everyone, as follows.

Long Run Planning Coalition Fundraising Plan

Premise: All fundraising efforts will be related to the organization's mission. The goals that the organization chooses in order to fulfill its mission will be created by the board of directors, with input from the membership and the staff. Foundation funding will help meet the goals set by the organization and not vice versa. Other fundraising programs will be improved as follows:

Membership

1. We will send a survey to the membership to determine their understanding of our work and mission. Once we see what people think about us, we will aim our newsletter and any other public relations materials to raising our visibility and clarifying our goals.

2. We will raise annual membership dues to at least $10 within the next two years.

3. We will send members two appeal letters per year asking for extra gifts for specific projects. Those who feel they are paying little to be members may be willing to give bigger gifts to these appeals. The letters will also help educate them and give them a greater sense of ownership in the group.

The Auction

1. We will set minimum bids for each item, equal to at least half the market value of the item. Our goal is to sell 90% of the items at 75% or more of their value.

2. When soliciting auction items, we will explain to the prospective donor that many items are sold for slightly less than their market value as a way to encourage local people to buy things or go on trips and weekend getaways that are normally aimed at tourists. We will make sure the prospective donor is comfortable with that premise.

3. At the auction, we will have a table with literature about Long Run and a banner with our mission statement on it hung prominently. The person who introduces the auctioneer will talk about Long Run's work for one or two minutes at the beginning of the auction and again in the middle. We will make sure the attendees understand that this is a *fundraising* event, not a midnight madness sale.

4. We will have a sign-in sheet and send a mail appeal to anyone who signs in who isn't already a member.

5. We will create another event with a low admission price that is strictly for fun. It will have food, drink and music. This event will please those who come to the auction strictly to socialize.

Long Run has now implemented this plan, and for the last two years has more than doubled their income from membership and events to $50,000. There were no complaints from members when dues went up, and more members have volunteered than ever before. Several have said that they are pleased that Long Run seems to be doing more organizing. Ironically, Long Run is not doing more, but they are much more visible. They have put some of the money they are raising into a reserve fund and are contemplating doing a big organizing campaign. Their foundation support remains strong.

Their auction continues to be very successful. They have lost some of the die-hard bargain hunters, but have gained people looking for quality items. Much to the surprise of the group, many items are selling at their full market value, and some at even higher prices. Moreover, the people they are attracting to the auction like Long Run and want to support their work. A number of auction attendees have become regular donors.

Successful fundraising requires first and foremost being comfortable with money — asking for it, having it and spending it, and assigning a monetary value to items for sale. Our classist society will not be changed by charging too little for events or by feeling uncomfortable with offering premiums on direct mail appeals. If you start every discussion about events, dues, products or fees with the seven questions outlined above, and frame the discussion in the context of your mission, the friends and the money you make will both serve to advance your goals.

twelve

Collaborative Fundraising

Collaborative fundraising is an idea that gets talked about a great deal, but there are surprisingly few examples of it working. In practice, it occurs on both a formal and informal level. At the formal level, collaborative fundraising has been institutionalized by federated funds like the Black United Fund, the various Community Shares, and the United Way. Other examples include public foundations like the Funding Exchange, RESIST, and the Astraea National Lesbian Action Foundation. All of these organizations raise money from a variety of donors and direct it to service or social justice work. At a more informal level, social change groups can collaborate on fundraising in a variety of ways.

Here are three successful examples of collaborative fundraising, followed by a discussion of what makes collaboration successful and how it can go wrong.

CASE STUDIES

Equipment

Three groups located on the same floor of a downtown office building all need new office equipment. Their budgets range from $75,000 to $150,000 and they have a total of six full-time staff among them. They decide to compile a joint list of their equipment needs and consider what can be shared by all three groups and what each group must own itself. They decide they could share a fancy copy machine, a laptop computer for any staff to use when travelling, and two laser printers. Each staff person needs their own upgraded computer and each group needs its own new fax machine. They include all these needs in a proposal to a family foundation that has previously funded each of them for various programs. The foundation is so pleased by this vision of sharing high-quality equipment that they not only fund the entire request, they also give the groups money for a refrigerator and a new couch for the groups' joint kitchen.

A Webmaster

Five groups working on a variety of social justice issues all want to use their Web sites more effectively. Four of the groups have been relying on the volunteer efforts of board members and other volunteers to maintain their sites, and one group has a staff person who is supposed to spend four hours a week on the site but never finds the time. Three of the groups have attractive Web sites but they rarely have time to update them and the sites have no interactive features. When staff from the groups see each other at various meetings, they discuss what they can do to take advantage of this technology. Through these discussions they develop the idea of hiring a full-time Webmaster who would spend the equivalent of one day a week working on each group's Web site.

Each group puts up $7,000 for the salary and benefits of this person. Each organization provides him with information so he can make the sites more interesting. He also develops a different fundraising pitch on each site. He links all the sites to each other and seeks links to other nonprofit groups. Soon, the Web sites have a lot more traffic and the groups feel this has been a very good investment. The Webmaster had planned to do this work as a freelancer, but finds having a regular salary and benefits much easier than constantly looking for work. He does not have a set day for each group, so he is accessible to all the groups as they need him.

A Joint Phone-a-Thon

Three groups in a large city decide to conduct a joint phone-a-thon. One group organizes tenants, the second provides high-quality, low-cost childcare, and the third offers free legal services to poor people. The phone-a-thon can take advantage of the strengths of each group: the tenants' rights group has a lot of volunteers but little money; the childcare group has a large space, little money and volunteers who are already doing as much as they can; the legal services group has some extra money, but few volunteers.

The legal services group pays for a bank of 10 phones to be hooked up at the childcare facility for two weekday evenings and one weekend. The tenant organization's volunteers coordinate and do most of the calling, using lists supplied by the three groups. The childcare center is open during the day for people to drop their checks off, which many donors elect to do, and some of the volunteers there help to address envelopes and write thank-you notes to people who pledge on the phone. The callers are trained in a rap from each group and call on behalf of whichever group the prospect's name came from. In other words, the lapsed donors from the childcare center are asked to donate to that group, the people on the legal services list are called on behalf of that group, and likewise for the tenants' rights group. The callers have to be trained, but enjoy learning about these other two groups.

Each donation received is allocated to the appropriate group. The legal services group nets the least income because they incurred the highest cost, but they are the most pleased of the three groups because they got a number of new and renewing donors with almost no volunteer effort and they got to test how well their group would "sell" by phone. The tenants' rights group is very happy because they break even on the phone-a-thon and they now have a trained cadre of people comfortable with making these phone calls. The childcare center is the least happy, as they contributed both the space and some volunteer effort and had the lowest return from their prospect list. Nonetheless, they feel it was worth the effort.

WHAT IT TAKES TO COLLABORATE

As you can see, these collaborative fundraising efforts differ significantly. One is a straightforward one-time request to a funder, the second is an ongoing joint commitment to a staff person, and the third is a fairly complicated sharing of time and money in an elaborate event. In each case, however, certain things were in place for the joint fundraising effort to work. If you are considering a collaborative fundraising effort, take note of the following conditions:

1. *Most important, the reward for the joint effort must be greater than if each group had attempted the strategy on their own.* In our examples, the first set of groups got better and more equipment than they likely could have asked for independently; the second set of groups got better staffing than if they had each simply contracted with a freelance person for eight hours a week; and the third set of groups was able to engage in a strategy that none of them could have done alone.

2. *The groups should have similar values and they should like each other.* Ideally, groups will have worked together on other efforts. This is particularly important when the outcome may vary from group to group, as in the phone-a-thon example. Although the childcare center wasn't as happy with the effort as the other two groups, they did not feel cheated or that the callers had not done well with their prospects.

3. *The division of money and labor must be decided ahead of the effort.* In the first case, the division is straightforward. In the second, the groups must trust that the staff person will give each group their fair share of time and attention. In the third case, although the expenses of the phone-a-thon could be anticipated, the donations raised could not be predicted. However, each group had an equal opportunity to train the callers and solicited donations from its own list.

4. Each group should contribute its strength to the effort. Groups must think creatively about their joint effort so that each is offering a part they can do well.

5. Authority must be established. Each group must assign a point person who has a reasonable amount of authority to make decisions for the whole group. Lines of authority and division of labor must be clear, particularly if the groups are not dividing the work evenly.

6. All agreements must be in writing. There should be a brief statement of the rationale for each part of the agreement and, in the case of ongoing collaborations, a statement of how and by whom the results will be evaluated and under what circumstances the agreement can be dissolved. These agreements are contractual and need to be approached seriously and thoughtfully, with as many people involved in creating the agreement as will be involved in implementing it.

FAILED COLLABORATIONS

Now let's look at two examples of collaborations that failed and what might have been done to anticipate or resolve the problems the groups faced.

Fred, Marta and Eiko

Two five-year-old grassroots community organizations decide that their budgets and workload are large enough to require a part-time development director. The executive directors of both groups, Fred and Marta, are friends and have discussed the fact that most of their time is now devoted to fundraising, to the neglect of their groups' organizing efforts. As neither group can afford a full-time person, they decide to create a shared full-time position, which enables them to offer a livable wage and benefits. They hire Eiko, who has little experience and a lot of enthusiasm. Eiko will work Monday, Tuesday and Wednesday morning for Fred's group, then walk down the street and spend the rest of the week with Marta's organization. Fred and Marta have been through enough organizational drama to take precautions. They sit down with Eiko and discuss potential problems and how to avoid them. They make agreements about what will happen if there is a conflict in fundraising deadlines and Eiko can meet only one, or if Eiko has to go to a meeting for Group A on her Group B day, and what will happen if one group likes her and the other doesn't. They work out as many policies as possible and make a commitment to keep the lines of communication open.

However, the one thing they don't discuss is what ultimately foils the plan, which is that Eiko eventually is happier working for one group than the other. After about six months, Eiko realizes that she looks forward to going to work at Fred's group, but not Marta's. There are a number of reasons for this. Fred is easier to talk with; Marta is often not in the office, and when she is, she seems impatient. Eiko feels disrespected by the organizers at Marta's group, who barely acknowledge her, and by the chair of the board, who always says to her, "Hope you are earning your keep," or "I don't see any checks on your desk." When Eiko complains, Marta tells her not to be so sensitive.

The chair of Fred's board, on the other hand, is a development director in another organization. She has lunch with Eiko every two weeks and makes herself available to answer questions. Fundraising is much more part of the culture at Fred's group and the organizers on staff offer to help, and often bring ideas to Eiko. They like her and include her in their conversations and even their social plans. Her work is paying off for both groups but because Fred's board is more involved in fundraising, his group is raising more money. Marta attributes this to Eiko working harder for Fred than for her.

Because all three of these people are able to be honest, this situation does not continue very long. Eiko asks for a meeting with both directors and says that she wishes to work full-time for Fred and quit working for Marta. Even if Fred cannot afford her or does not wish to hire her, she wishes to leave Marta's group. Marta is disappointed and a little hurt, but agrees that Eiko should not work for her group any longer if she doesn't want to. Fred is pleased because he thinks Eiko does a great job.

Two years later, Eiko is still with Fred, and Marta's group has seen four half-time development people come and go.

Unspoken Assumptions

The PTAs from four city schools decide to do a walkathon together and share the proceeds equally. Each PTA has sponsored a walkathon in the past and believes that they will raise more money in a joint event than by having four separate ones. One person from each PTA is assigned to be the point person, and those four people, with four others, form the planning committee. They are to distribute fliers in the schools, get the teachers excited about the event, plan the route, involve the kids in signing up to walk and get pledges, and so on. Trouble arises immediately. A member of the PTA for the most affluent school complains that the route planned goes through "bad neighborhoods, too dangerous for children." The parent who planned the route replies, "That's my neighborhood where I am raising my kids." The route stays as planned, but tension remains.

A point person from one of the poorer schools proves to be unreliable. She is always late to meetings, she forgets to give out fliers and doesn't follow through on other commitments. One member of the committee attributes her unreliability to the fact that she is a single mother, which offends three others on the committee who are single parents. By the day of the walkathon, only two members of the committee are on speaking terms with the whole committee, but the walkathon goes well anyway. It raises $6,000, which is $1,500 more than their combined totals previously.

As it turns out, the two poorest schools have raised the most money. The smallest produced the most walkers, while the affluent school produced the least money and the fewest walkers, although they did no worse than in the past. The three poorer and smaller schools now resent sharing the money equally with the more affluent school. The discussion at the follow-up meeting goes as follows:

Affluent school point person: "We made this agreement to share the proceeds equally and we should keep it. This is how the cookie crumbles."

Small school point person, "Don't you mean the designer cookie?"

Poor school point person 1: "You are a fine one to talk, since it is just a miracle that your school participated at all."

Poor school point person 2, pointing to the first two speakers: "If you had any honor at all, you would give us two-thirds of the money and split the other third between you."

Affluent school person: "If you had any honor you would stick with the agreement."

In the end, with much grumbling, they all decide to honor their original agreement and they split the money evenly. However, they never do anything jointly again.

GETTING HINDSIGHT TO BE FORESIGHT

Let's look at what went wrong in these two experiences and how it could have been anticipated, or avoided.

In the first case, although Marta's and Fred's groups seemed similar, they were actually quite different. They both did community organizing and they both had overworked directors, but Fred's group was much more ready to have a development director. Marta did not wish to make the time to supervise such a person, nor was she willing to provide the education required to help board members and staff understand the role of a development director. Moreover, no one else on the board had this understanding. Had Eiko had more experience, she might have been able to provide that education herself and she would not have needed Marta as much. However, without strong support from an executive director, even the strongest and most experienced development person is going to have a hard time.

In the case of the four PTAs, we see four similar groups working on an event they are all familiar with, where the work can be divided fairly evenly. However, a second look shows very different groups. Class bias, unspoken assumptions that the affluent school would raise as much or more money than the other schools, and lack of accountability for the volunteers on the part of each PTA led to a bad experience. Ironically, in terms of money raised, this collaboration meets our first rule that the efforts of the combined groups must yield substantially more than their single efforts added together. However, the bad feelings generated early on by the other problems could not be overcome by the good outcome.

When deciding on any collaboration, it is important to brainstorm all the worst things that could possibly happen and then decide what you are going to do about them. Death, natural disaster, irreconcilable differences, dishonesty, incompetence, or a desire to disband the joint effort before it is completed are the most common things to discuss. Division of work and resources should be spelled out in great detail. In joint fundraising efforts, it is far more often the case that the poorer groups, the poorer neighborhoods or the poorer people will raise more money than their richer counterparts. Differences in groups' budgets, their access to money or perception of access to money can complicate but do not have to undermine collaborations if they are acknowledged at the start.

Overall, the benefits of undertaking collaborative fundraising efforts far outweigh the risks, but because of the risks, groups must enter collaborative relationships seriously and with thorough, honest discussion on the part of all the people who will be involved.

Some Ways Organizations Have Collaborated to Raise or Save Money

■ ■ ■ ■ ■ ■ ■ ■ ■ ■ ■ ■ ■ ■ ■ ■ ■

1. Discounts for guaranteed spending/patronage.
   - Several organizations whose staff travel a lot use the same travel agent in exchange for a 1% reduction in commissions.
   - Another set of community groups supports their local office supply store rather than buying from a chain. In return, they receive a 10–15% discount as long as the groups maintain a certain dollar amount in purchases.

2. Two groups that have offices in the same building share a conference room. Since it goes unused most evenings and weekends, they have begun to rent it out and share the proceeds. They take turns with the clean-up and they share the advertising and booking tasks, which are fairly minimal.

3. Over the years, many groups have wanted me to train their board members in how to ask for money. Often one organization will invite two or three groups that are similar to them and split my fee and expenses. This gives all the groups more personalized training than would be available at a much larger workshop and has the advantage of allowing board members to hear objections and questions from board members of other groups.

4. One group processes donations made by credit card for themselves and three other groups. This produces the volume needed to use credit cards for donations and lowers the fees for doing so for each group. The group doing the accounting takes a small fee for their effort. Donors using credit cards to make their gift are told, "Your donation will show up on your charge card as Good Group." This service is best if limited to not more than five organizations or the work of keeping up with it will be more than the profit it generates.

thirteen

Fundraising for the Long Haul

At the end of a three-day workshop that I thought had gone well, a participant came up to me and asked, "Aren't there easier ways to raise money than what we have covered here?" I searched her face for some sign that she was pulling my leg, but she looked quite sincere and there was no sarcasm in her tone, so I asked her what she meant. "I mean there must be easier ways to get money than having to ask for it over and over and keep all these records and do all this planning. This is going to take a lot of time."

I realized she was serious so I gave her a serious reply. I told her that there are ways in which fundraising could be easier. For example, the government could use our taxes to provide universal health care, high-quality public schools, free universities, cheap and efficient public transportation, child care facilities and the like. Instead, we have a bloated military budget that is larger than the military budgets of the next nine most-militarized nations combined. If the government funded education, child care, social services and health care, nonprofits that provide those services wouldn't have to raise money from the private sector. Furthermore, the tax system could be designed so that corporations paid their fair share of taxes, and capital gains taxes could at least equal income taxes. My participant took notes as I talked, so I continued.

I told her that in such a system, all taxpayers could be allowed to deduct their charitable giving from their taxes, which would mean that the majority of taxpayers (who do not itemize) would receive the same benefits for their charitable giving as the minority of itemizers do now. Put more baldly, poor people would receive the same tax treatment for their charitable giving as those who are much better off.

I ended by saying "Besides these and other structural changes, there are no easier ways to raise money that I know of."

She stopped taking notes, nodded her head sadly and wandered off.

I don't know why this participant thought I would deliberately teach hard ways to raise money and keep the easy ways to myself. But I think many organizations wish fundraising were a chore like brushing your teeth — you do it two or three times a day but only for a few minutes — then spit, rinse and it's over.

But it's not such a simple task, so organizations that raise money need to focus on those aspects of fundraising that are fun, even wonderful, profound and life changing.

It is true that many things about fundraising are tedious, such as stuffing envelopes or sitting in meetings with people who seem to be paid for the number of words that come out of their mouth. Some aspects of fundraising require intense concentration on minute details, such as data entry or checking the names of donors listed in the Annual Report against the list printed out from your database.

Asking a friend for a donation, making a phone call to a generous but cantankerous donor, investing money in a strategy that you hope will make back the money you spent and much more are aspects of fundraising that can be anxiety provoking. And the constant work of keeping the money coming in can wear down the most dedicated person and the most durable organization.

But many organizations do mount successful fundraising campaigns year after year and the most successful organizations do it with enthusiasm and creativity. To stay in fundraising for a long time requires discipline and training your mind in the habit of thinking about the positive aspects of fundraising. This is not a false or rose-colored-glasses way of thinking — it is just making choices about what to focus on.

So, when you think about fundraising, think of the fun parts, such as being in meetings with people who are smart and creative and like to laugh, planning the next issue of the newsletter or setting goals for next year. Remember the exhilaration at the end of a successful special event, when you know that everyone had a good time, that it made money and brought in new people, and that all the hard work paid off. Think of the sense of accomplishment in board members who have asked for money in person for the first time and whose good experience makes them look forward to asking the next person.

Consider the times when organizations make very brave decisions, trusting that the money will continue nonetheless: a church that decides to publicly welcome gay men and lesbians even though it may lose its biggest contributors; a community organization determined to challenge the labor practices of a powerful local corporation even though it may get caught up in expensive lawsuits; a health clinic that continues to offer abortion services even though the government has withdrawn all funds from clinics that perform abortions.

Most of all, focus on the experience of the extraordinary generosity of all kinds of people. The janitor who gave $1,500 to the capital campaign of a local theater group when it was evicted and had to find new performance space; the school teacher who gives $250 a year to a rape crisis center; the heir to a real estate fortune who gave away all his money (almost $1,000,000) and now works as a receptionist for a public interest law firm. (These are all true stories.) There are thousands more stories from the 70% of adults who give away money.

Serious fundraising also means that you will have very serious conversations with donors. Will child molesting ever cease to exist? Is it too late to save the environment? Can children be raised free of sex stereotypes? How can racism be eradicated?

As a fundraiser, you will be in the middle of all of it — the fun, the serious, the scary and the profound. As an organization, you will go through it all. Raising money is hard work to be sure, but not having money is even harder. Those are your choices.

I have tried to share what it means to raise money year in and year out. Keeping a fundraising program going and expanding is very different from starting one. Just as in a relationship, the initial excitement of a new organization has a life of its own; after a few years, that excitement has to be cultivated and nurtured. There are many organizations that have been around for a lot of years, and that is their main accomplishment. But if your organization is to grow old, in the sense that cultures who have respect for age use the word, it cannot just stay open and survive year after year. Engaging in frequent self-examination through planning and evaluation, welcoming new ideas and people, and taking risks are the hallmarks of vibrant and dynamic organizations.

Nonprofits that work for social change must themselves be agents of change. The ways we think about money, raise it, spend it, save it, invest it, and plan for it are some of the most basic elements for modeling the world we want to create.

Bibliography

Other Titles in the Chardon Press Series:

- *Ask and You Shall Receive: Leader Manual,* Kim Klein
- *Fundraising for Social Change,* Kim Klein
- *Grassroots Grants: An Activist's Guide to Proposal Writing,* Andy Robinson
- *Inspired Philanthropy: Creating a Giving Plan,* Tracy Gary and Melissa Kohner
- *Making Policy, Making Change,* Makani N. Themba
- *Raise More Money: The Best of the Grassroots Fundraising Journal,* Kim Klein and Stephanie Roth, Editors
- *Roots of Justice: Stories of Organizing in Communities of Color,* Larry R. Salomon

OTHER USEFUL TITLES:

Achieving Excellence in Fundraising, by Henry Rosso and Associates. SF: Jossey Bass Publishers, 1991. $42.95.

Beyond Fund Raising: New Strategies for Nonprofit Innovation and Investment, by Kay Sprinkel Grace. NY: John Wiley & Sons, 1997. $29.95.

Faith and Philanthropy in America, by Robert Wuthnow, Virginia A. Hodgkinson and Associates. SF: Jossey-Bass, Publishers, 1990. $39.95.

Giving USA: Annual Report on Philanthropy, AAFRC Trust for Philanthropy (10293 North Meridian St., Suite 175, Indianapolis, IN 46290). $45 per year.

Grassroots and Nonprofit Leadership, by Berit Lakey, George Lakey, Rod Napier, and Janice Robinson. New Society Publishers (4527 Springfield Ave., Philadelphia, PA 19143). $16.95.

Grassroots Fundraising: The Kim Klein Video Series. (Order from Headwaters Fund, 122 W. Franklin Ave, Suite 518, Minneapolis, MN 55404, or call 612/879-0602.) Purchase price is .1% of organization's annual budget (minimum $25, maximum $499).

The Grassroots Fundraising Book, by Joan Flanagan. Contemporary Books (180 North Michigan Avenue, Chicago, IL 60601), 1992. $16.95.

Holding the Center: America's Nonprofit Sector at a Crossroads, by Lester M. Salamon. The Nathan Cummings Foundation (1926 Broadway, Suite 600, New York, NY 10023; 212/787-7300), 1997. Single copies free.

How to Produce Fabulous Fundraising Events: Reap Remarkable Returns with Minimal Effort, by Betty Stallings and Donna McMillion. Pleasanton, CA: Building Better Skills (1717 Courtney Ave, Suite 201, Pleasanton, CA 94588; 925/426-8335), 1999. $30.

Leadership and the New Science: Discovering Order in a Chaotic World, by Margaret Wheatley. Berrett-Koehler, San Francisco, CA, 1999. $24.95.

Managing the NonProfit Organization: Principles and Practices, by Peter Drucker. NY: HarperCollins, 1990. $13.50.

The Nonprofit Manager's Resource Directory, by Ronald A. Landskroner. NY: John Wiley & Sons, 1996. $69.95.

Raising Money by Mail: Strategies for Growth and Financial Stability, by Mal Warwick. Berkeley, CA: Strathmoor Press (2550 Ninth Street, Suite 1000, Berkeley, CA 94710-2516), 1996. $24.95.

The Second Legal Answer Book for Nonprofit Organizations, by Bruce R. Hopkins. NY: John Wiley & Sons, 1998. $79.95.

Special Events: Proven Strategies for Nonprofit Fundraising, by Alan Wendroff. NY: John Wiley & Sons, 1999. $30.

Strategic Planning for Nonprofit Organizations, by Michael Allison and Judy Kaye. NY: John Wiley and Sons, 1997. $39.95.

Successful Fundraising: A Complete Handbook for Volunteers and Professionals, by Joan Flanagan, Contemporary Books (180 North Michigan Avenue, Chicago, IL 60601), 1993. $19.95.

Successful Fundraising for Arts and Cultural Organizations, by Karen Brooks Hopkins and Carolyn Stolper Friedman. Phoenix: Oryx Press. (4041 North Central, Phoenix, AZ 85012-3397), 1996. $34.95

ALSO CONTACT:

National Center for Nonprofit Boards: www.ncnb.org, or call 800/883-6262 for a catalog with all of their excellent information.

Index

RESOURCES FOR SOCIAL CHANGE

AVAILABLE FROM JOSSEY-BASS AND CHARDON PRESS

Raise More Money
The Best of the Grassroots Fundraising Journal

Kim Klein and
Stephanie Roth, Editors
Paper 208 pages
ISBN 0-7879-6175-2 $28.00

This collection offers a wealth of tips and strategies, as well as guidance on how small nonprofits can raise money from their communities, reduce their dependence on foundations or corporations, and develop long-term financial stability.

Fundraising for Social Change
FOURTH EDITION

Kim Klein

Paper 416 pages
ISBN 0-7879-6174-4 $35.00

This classic how-to fundraising text teaches you what you need to know to raise money from individuals. Learn how to set fundraising goals based on realistic budgets; write successful direct mail appeals; produce special events; raise money from major gifts, planned giving, capital campaigns, and more.

Grassroots Grants
An Activist's Guide to Proposal Writing

Andy Robinson
Paper 208 pages
ISBN 0-7879-6177-9 $25.00

The author describes just what it takes to win grants, including how grants fit into your complete fundraising program, how to use your grant proposal as an organizing plan, how to design fundable projects, how to build your proposal piece by piece, and more.

Ask and You Shall Receive
A Fundraising Training Program for Religious Organizations and Projects

Kim Klein
Paper
ISBN 0-7879-5563-9 $23.00

A self-study course in the basics of grassroots fundraising written specifically for groups raising funds for religious organizations and projects. (Includes a Leader Manual and a Participant Manual.)

Inspired Philanthropy
Creating a Giving Plan
Tracy Gary and Melissa Kohner
Paper 128 pages
ISBN 0-7879-6176-0 $20.00

Learn how to match your giving with your values. No matter how much or little you have to give, you'll learn how to create a giving plan that will make your charitable giving catalytic.

TO ORDER, CALL (800) 956-7739 OR VISIT US AT
www.josseybass.com/go/chardonpress